THE
ROAD RIDER

THE
ROAD RIDER

A GUIDE TO ON-THE-ROAD MOTORCYCLING

by
ROBIN PERRY

CROWN PUBLISHERS, INC.   NEW YORK

Inquiries should be addressed to Crown Publishers, Inc.,
419 Park Avenue South, New York, N.Y. 10016.

Library of Congress Catalog Card Number: 73–91519
Printed in the United States of America
Published simultaneously in Canada by
General Publishing Company Limited

Design: Dennis Critchlow
Second Printing, November, 1974

Dedication

In Memoriam
Neal Chann, died December 23, 1973

There are people in this world whose total life is dedicated to one idea and ideal, and their fierce loyalty to this chosen theme shames the rest of us who happily or not drift through life enjoying the fruits and benefits of the true idealists.

Neal Chann was one of those idealists, who ate, slept, and believed totally in motorcycles and motorcycling. A Honda, Kawasaki, Husqvarna, and Penton dealer in Groton, Connecticut, he ran his business with the same ethic that he lived by: that he would sell only quality products and that he would service what he sold.

Neal was a concerned motorcycle dealer, concerned with the new driver, concerned with safety, concerned with the environment. Actively supporting motorcycle racing in all its forms, Neal Chann was a true motorcycle sportsman and worthy of this small dedication.

Acknowledgments

First, to George Strong for his endless willingness to be available for picture-taking sessions at the oddest times. It is George who posed for most of the photographs and on a variety of motorcycles.

Next, to Sally Rice, my gal Friday, who typed, retyped, and typed again, who listened to my reading over and over again, and finally, who spurred me on when I lagged behind my schedule, my heartfelt thanks.

To Jack Mercer, Mr. Motorcycle to me, who had faith in me before I did, and whose help and support made it easier for me to get cooperation.

And finally, to Ralph Strong, for putting up with the many inconveniences caused by my need for information or the loan of a bike for a photograph. His gentle humor and great understanding are appreciated.

In Appreciation to the Following Dealers:

Neal Chann, J. N. C. Motors, Groton, Connecticut

Ralph Strong, Ralph Strong Motorcycles, Waterford, Connecticut

Don Werner, New London County Motorcycles, Groton, Connecticut

Contents

A double disc brake on a Suzuki. This is a front wheel with one of the best brake assemblies made.

Introduction

"WHY A MOTORCYCLE?"

Man *and his machine, pit-*
ting themselves against the elements
A hero in the twentieth century
He steps outside his house, casually glances up at the
sky with a weathered eye
flips his cigarette to the ground as he pulls on his
gauntlets
throws one leg over his mount
a powerful kick and he lights up his charger with a roar
While she is warming up he buckles the safety strap on
his helmet
checks his gussets and zippers and listens to the sweet
purring
of his engine as she smooths out

1

touches his handlebar grips with a gentle caress
the affection known only to a knight of old
He throws in his clutch, kicks it in gear, and lets it out
with a head-snapping twist
Out into the wind and the sun into the valley of
    conquerors
Riding his charger at gutsy half throttle
He feels the blood pulsing through his veins
the hair on his scalp rising as the wind whistles about
    his helmet
his muscles come alive as he skillfully whips around the
    curve at 30°
adjusting his weight, settling in his seat on a steed
of chromium and Candy Apple Red

What is it that makes us men, one and all, young and old, into bright-eyed little boys when we see the latest shiny two-wheeler at our local motorcycle shop?

Are we little boys again? Are we playing with choochoo trains, toy soldiers, or model airplanes? What is this complete fascination that reduces us to eager young kids when we see the latest Super Sport? Is it a love object? A phallic symbol? A test of our manhood? A manifestation of our hero fantasies? Yes, it as all of these things because riding a motorcycle excites a man as no other sport can. This is attested to by the fact that there are over ten million registered vehicles in the United States today and this figure is expected to double by 1980.

What is this obsession with the motorcycle?
It is the ultimate in control
It is man challenging the elements,
the wind, and even the rain and snow
There is no other thrill like feeling the pulse
of a well-tuned motorcycle between your legs
your hands firmly in control of your handlebar grips,
the smooth rhythm of the highway
pulsing and vibrating beneath you
To feel the mastery that you alone
and only you can feel at that moment.
A slight twist of the throttle and you are off
with an acceleration that belies the motorcycle's size
because it can outstrip any car

The twist of the hips and the quick weave around a
    sharp S turn
The tingle of leaning over with danger so close yet so
    remote
Gritting the teeth and the urge to roll on the throttle to
    its fullest stop,
to fly off into the sky
right into the clouds and sun
the feel of the saddle as it gives with every stretch of
    road,
the sharp intake of clean cold air
that fills your blood with an exhilaration no other thing
    can
Quivering, vibrating, the tautness,
yet the relaxation of your muscles,
but at the ready,
quickening to speed faster and faster
until you can sense yourself flying off into space
the smooth response, the quick braking
the downshift as she responds to every touch
even slowing down and braking can be a maneuver of
    great thrill
Sometimes the lazy country road drive
looking at the countryside for the first time,
you feel akin to nature once again
Just as a little boy you used to walk these roads—the
    complete serenity
you are not lonely, you and your machine
You have a lot in common,
but where does machine leave off and man begin?

I can't put into words all of the varied magnificent feelings that I have enjoyed on motorcycles for the past forty years. Today's modern *four*-wheel vehicles drive me, but I drive my motorcycle. There is a personal relationship that develops between man and his motorcycle, and he jealously guards this even from his other loved ones. Perhaps the motorcycle is the counterpart of the eighteenth century horse. It satisfies the rider's ego. It represents a challenge to him. Driving it with skill is the mark of the creative artist. He tries to shift without being pitched forward or snapped backward. He smoothly applies his brakes and decelerates with his engine to see how smoothly he can slow down. He tries to come to a stop with his feet up before he puts them down to balance his machine "paddling," the mark of a sissy rider. The air in his lungs is exhilarating, the wind in his face snaps him to attention, he hugs his machine for comfort and warmth, a loving pat on the tank; "We'll make it, won't we, ole girl."

A dashing heroic figure, yes. In this twentieth century world of concrete, steel, and machinery, do not fold, mutilate or spindle, his motorcycle represents his escape, his alter ego. He is a knight in shining armor again. He draws attention when he rides down the street, see how they turn and stare in envy, the girls with admiration, perhaps; but he is noticed. In a way, isn't that what it is all about? Don't we all want to be noticed just a little bit?

Why a motorcycle?

I don't know why. Just because it is all these things to us and many more I am not articulate enough to tell you about, but that is why a motorcycle.

1

Which Motorcycle
Do I Buy?

A FAIR question. Like everything else that you buy, you have to determine what you want to do with it. If you intend to tool around the backcountry roads, anywhere between 100cc to 250cc has sufficient power. If you are going to find yourself out on a turnpike, freeway, or limited access highway, you had better think in terms of 350cc and up. If you are going to tour and travel great distances with a passenger, you'd better think of a 450cc to a 1000cc.

Mechanically all modern road bikes are highly sophisticated and almost foolproof. The Japanese machines are marvels of engineering know-how. The Yamaha, Honda, Kawasaki, and Suzuki are four of the better known. The English are known for their Triumph, BSA, and Norton lines, and the German

BMW has a road-riding reputation that has never been surpassed. Here in the United States the Harley-Davidson still ranks as the granddaddy of the big ones. A fast machine coming up is the Moto Guzzi from Italy. These are but a few of the available machines.

Each of these manufacturers make a full line usually running from 100cc to 750cc. Most of the modern machines are 2-cylinder, some 3, some 4. Some manufacturers like Yamaha and Honda make one or more. Most 4-cylinders are 4-strokes.

First determine what you want to do with your machine, and if you say turnpike and maybe a passenger, start your thinking in terms of 350cc. If price is a consideration and you can't afford it, my suggestion is don't go to a lesser "cc" but to a secondhand machine from a reliable dealer.

This brings up the dealer. When you buy from an individual, you have little or no recourse in the event anything goes wrong. When you buy from a reputable dealer, you might pay a little bit more but the dealers that I know stand behind their motorcycles. The average 30-day warranty is 50–50–30. This means the dealer will pay 50 percent of parts and labor guarantee on a used machine for 30 days. This is pretty standard in the motorcycle industry. Of course, this doesn't take into consideration the fact that some dealers will stand behind some broken part and the labor to replace it when the trouble recurs time and time again. These situations are rare and, of course, they are subject to negotiation. If the dealer has a very good client who has purchased previous machines and he expects to sell more to the same person, he's inclined to bend a bit. If you buy secondhand, try to stay as near to the current year as possible. Motorcycle importation regulations have been changing rapidly, requiring more and more safety devices. Mechanical innovations are almost radical year by year. So what do you look for?

If you have the bread, go for the biggest machine you can afford, in the area of 350cc to 750cc. This for a number of reasons. One is, most everybody that buys a light machine trades it in in short order and "upgrades" himself. It's downright frightening not to be able to pass on a turnpike, and new riders find themselves exploring newer and wider horizons, which sooner or later brings them into contact with the Interstate or turnpike. When you are out there on the Interstate and you pass that mother truck and you have to struggle and strain to make your bike pass, imagine what it would be like with a 100-pound woman on the back.

New regulations call for very large taillights, directional signals front and rear, larger brakes, better headlights; believe me, you need them.

Two- or 4-cycle? Two-cycles whine a little bit and the biggest complaint was that you used to have to mix your oil and gas; nowadays there are automatic adjustment pumping mechanisms that meter the oil into the engine as it is needed. If you are buying a secondhand machine, look for this type of lubrication; if you have to "hand mix" oil and gas, you're going to be limited in range. You are also out of date. Modern 2-cycle machines are very reliable. Every bit as reliable as the 4-cycle.

Two, 3, 4 cylinders or one? Definitely at least 2. Most road machines are 2 cylinders anyway; the singles are great woods machines.

Shaft-drive-motor Moto Guzzi. Shaft drives prevent a lot of the problems of adjusting chain and with very little maintenance, but they are heavy and cost extra. This is one of two bikes that use the shaft as this is written. Note the passenger's handrail. Pretty good—at least it isn't in back— but it is still best to hang on to the driver.

How about a Combo bike? Sort of a "Street Scrambler." Not recommended. Half-road, half-woods generally gives you a half-baked bike. If you are going to be touring or doing a lot of road riding or using this for transportation, my suggestion is to stick with a road bike. They are less "peaky."

Chain or shaft drive? The shaft drive is standard on bikes such as the BMW and the Moto Guzzi, and Honda and some of the others are playing around with a shaft drive that should be out next year. These are considered the most reliable. As far as advantage is concerned, the shaft drive requires no maintenance and little adjustment and is usually much cleaner, very rarely breaks down. Its disadvantages are weight and cost. The chain does require maintenance and constant adjustment; it can be messy. If you don't look after it on a long trip, you could lose it. On the other hand, a comparable chain machine to a shaft-driven one might be as much as $500 to $600 less. Are you willing to pay $500 or $600 for a shaft drive?

A motorcycle can brake better than a car. Almost all the modern road machines have disc brakes on the front wheel, some on both wheels. These give you unbelievable stopping power, definitely a plus feature. There is nothing wrong with the leading shoe type; it is just that disc brakes are where it is going to be.

Note "crash" or guard around radiator on Suzuki GT 750.

Comfort is a big item in buying a road bike, especially if you plan to do any touring. Riding comfort means good suspension and soft and adjustable saddle springs. You should be comfortable when you sit on the machine, and comfort is pretty hard to judge in the dealer's showroom. You reach forward and grip the handlebars and it doesn't feel like much of a strain, but after 50 miles in that position, your shoulder muscles will ache and your neck will think your head is falling off. See if you can sit comfortably in a semislouch position without your arms being extended so that your elbows are locked. If you can reach your handlebar grips loosely from this position and without being too far up on the tank, you may be fitted for that bike. The farther forward you are on the bike, the less you are going to enjoy the effect of good suspension. Most of this suspension is aimed at the middle of the saddle. If you are already a rider, the best way is to take it out on the highway—the dealer usually lets you do this to try it out. You can't go for a long drive, but you should be able to tell how you'll feel.

Vibration is fatiguing and motorcycles do vibrate. Some reach a point where the vibration smooths out and the ride becomes very enjoyable. It's really not annoying, unless you are on a very long trip, but I'd say that 50 miles can be very enervating on a bike that vibrates. Where is your tolerance and where is someone else's? This vibration is an important consideration when buying a motorcycle, especially a big one. In general, it can be said that the 4-cylinder motorcycles have less of this high-speed vibration, therefore are less fatiguing, a worthy consideration in your purchasing analysis.

Saddle height is important to short people or rather short-legged people. The average saddle height is 31 inches. If you are 5′7″ or under, this might mean that you are "tippy-toeing" to reach the ground. This can be very awkward especially with a heavy motorcycle at a stop sign or a stoplight.

Most state laws require a motor vehicle (including a motorcycle) to have a headlight that throws a beam 500 feet. Surprisingly, most motorcycles don't meet this regulation. Usually the bigger models with 12 volts will comply. It doesn't seem important until you are tooling along in the dark and you come upon an old muffler or a block of wood or an animal. Just a thought for 12 volts. In reading over projected legislation relative to the use of motorcycles, from various states,

Two things here. You should buy a bike that you can balance with your feet flat on the ground; otherwise the saddle height is too high. Secondly, when you come to a stop, the passenger should keep his or her feet up at all times. Never try to assist the driver by balancing.

one proposed motor-vehicle law that seems to stand out above all others is the regulation requiring that headlights remain on during daylight hours as a safety feature. This could cause problems with the smaller cc bikes whose electrical systems are scaled down and are quite adequate during running conditions, but stop and go traffic conditions can very quickly drain a small battery, especially a 6-volt one. Not all 12-volt battery systems are adequate either, so make certain, when you are considering which bike to buy and reading test reports, that there is a plus sign for the electrical system in the test report.

All modern motorcycles have a seat large enough for two people with foot pegs for the rear passenger. Just make sure your passenger's toes or heels don't hit a hot muffler from their normal position on the rear pegs. Many a rider has had to buy new vinyl boots for his passenger and scrape the melted stuff off his chrome mufflers.

Mufflers are not much of a consideration as far as noise is concerned anymore. Federal regulations require that all imports comply with a 93-decibel rating or lower and most do. In fact, modern machines are so quiet you can't hear them.

Those pipes get hot and some girls wear modern vinyl boots. If boots touch the pipe, they'll melt. Proper position is to keep your boot on the peg. If you're wearing high heels, use the ball of your foot. Keep your feet off that pipe.

New BMWs and Hondas, Yamahas, Suzukis, Kawasakis are so quiet that even the rider can't hear them. If you are buying a used bike, check the muffler system to see that it is quiet and hasn't been blown out or that straight pipes haven't been substituted by a hot rodder.

Shop around. At the time this book is being written, motorcycle prices are pretty stable. By this, I mean the dealer is getting what he is asking for the bike. This usually includes the manufacturer's suggested price plus a setup charge, a freight charge, and applicable sales taxes. If you have picked out a bike, it won't hurt to ask for a discount. You may save yourself the price of the tax or better. One of the best ways to buy a used bike is through the classified section of your local paper. Quite often, you will find somebody that is moving, getting out of the service, or has some sort of unfortunate financial problem that requires that he sell his bike quickly and for cash. If you are up on your bike prices or even if you're not, look for comparable used bikes at your local dealer's, check the prices, and then go to see the advertised motorcycle. Carefully look over the bike. If you are not mechanically inclined and you are not familiar with motorcycles, my suggestion is to hire a local mechanic to go with you to look it over. You may have to slip him $10 or $15, but it may save you an awful lot of grief. As I may have said before, you can get a lot of bargains this way. In new and used, the best buys seem to be in the 350cc range. Very carefully compare features. Some of the more modern and up-to-date features are:

1. Disc brake
2. Electric starter
3. Oil warning light
4. Ignition warning light
5. Omniphase counterbalance mechanisms
6. Chain oiler
7. Chain tensioner
8. Burned-out stoplight warning light
9. Automatic low-high beam headlight switchovers
10. Oil radiators
11. Solid state electronic ignition
12. Water-cooled radiator
13. 6 months/6,000 miles guaranty
14. Tire wear indicator
15. Brake lining wear indicator

Naturally, the smaller cc machines don't have all the features that the big boys do. Everything is smaller, lighter, or just not on the bike. Warranties are pretty important, but nobody really reads the fine print. One manufacturer, Suzuki, has a 12-month or 12,000-mile warranty. The fine print says: "Covers all internal parts of cylinder head block & transmission." What about the rest of the machine? I don't know. Questioning dealers, I get different answers. Warranty contracts are very carefully worded and much depends on the dealer-customer relationship. One thing is certain; buy a machine from a reputable dealer, one that is reasonably near where you are basing your machine. Service shouldn't really be a problem. Assuming you do your own light maintenance, you might not even need the dealer's services. I find that on the average, the motorcycles are better made than their 4-wheeled counterparts.

There are a few things that are inadequate or missing from all bikes. This may be just a matter of the writer's opinion, but I have yet to find a horn on any motorcycle that is anywhere near adequate. I could shout louder. Another thing that I personally like is safety bars. We used to call them "crash" bars. I like them because they protect the rider's legs in the event of a spill, but these are listed accessory items that I consider necessary. More about them later.

Some of the features that you will see in the future are automatic transmission, Wankel engines, and fuel injection. A shaft drive will be much more common in the next few years, and many of the features listed will be common even on the smallest of motorcycles.

Financing a road machine represents no problem. All modern banks and finance companies will take the paper. Finance rates are very high. Unlike automotive dealers, motorcycle dealers don't have a "floor plan." Although many motorcyclists do finance their motorcycles through their local bank, the dealers don't often get a kickback on interest rates as automotive dealers do. When you pay 13.62 percent interest on your car, a good 5 percent of that is kicked back to the dealer, so whenever you find yourself winning a bargain with the dealer's salesman, he is usually using the 5 or 6 percent cushion involved in the finance charges to bargain with.

Modern motorcycle dealers don't have this privilege with banks—yet, every dealer has his own pet bank that he has been putting his paper through. In many of these cases, though, you are required to have minimum liability insurance. Some state laws prohibit having a motorcycle without liability insurance. In the next few years this will be prevalent all over the country. Incidentally, in most states where "no fault" insurance is in effect, you will find that motorcycles are excluded for obvious reasons.

Passenger liability is not so common, yet it should be—especially in a road machine. It bears looking into anyway. For those of you who can only ride about six months out of the year, as in the northern half of the United States, most insurance companies will insure for six-month periods. If you are interested in saving some money and you do live in such a locality, this is something to investigate. There are many sections of the country, such as my own (I live in Connecticut), where I ride all year round as long as the roads aren't covered with snow. My cutoff point is 20°. Below that I find it too uncomfortable.

In previous paragraphs, I lightly touched on the various numbers of cylinders. Let's discuss it a little more in depth. At

A 3-cylinder with a Ram air system, another Suzuki. A powerful and good road bike. A good-looking yet practical rig.

the present time (1974) there are motorcycles being manufactured and commonly sold with 1, 2, 3, and 4 cylinders. Naturally, as there is an increase in the number of cylinders, there is an increase in the number of accessory mechanical parts for that extra cylinder, the main one being another carburetor. The first thing that comes to someone's mind is that the more cylinders you have, the more trouble you will experience keeping the engine in tune. To a degree, this is true; but the advantages outweigh the disadvantages here. Especially, when you are on a road bike on a long tour. When you get up to the 3- and 4-cylinder motorcycle, they are in the 650cc class or bigger and are obviously built for long-distance touring. There is a very distinct advantage to a larger number of cylinders: they give a much smoother, quieter, and more comfortable ride. Naturally, multiple carburetors are interlocked, and it is my experience that you won't have any more maintenance problems with 3 or 4 cylinders than you do with 2. As a matter of fact, it is an advantage to have 4 cylinders because you can at least run on 3, or have 3 cylinders and run on 2 under emergency conditions. If you are a neophyte mechanic, you shouldn't be fiddling with the carburetors anyway. Your gas mileage is less with the increased number of cylinders.

Almost any motorcycle can give you a high top speed, so top speed is never a consideration in buying one. On the turnpikes in the United States you can't very well use the top speeds that some machines can reach, such as the Harleys, Hondas, Kawasaki, BMW, Suzuki, Yamaha, Triumph, Norton, and so on—all of these having 750cc and above, clear 120 mph. What is important is regulations Part 375 Consumer Information of the National Highway Traffic Safety Administration. These regulations came into effect in 1972 and by the time you are reading this book every single manufacturer will have available for any consumer information pertaining to *Stopping Distance* and *Acceleration and Passing Ability,* the latter's covering: low-speed pass and high-speed pass. This information that must be given with every motorcycle represents the results obtainable by skilled drivers under controlled road and vehicle conditions. It *may not* be correct under other considerations.

Stopping Distance. This figure indicates the braking performance that can be met or exceeded by the vehicles to which it applies, without locking the wheels, under different conditions of loading and with partial failures of the braking system. They give you two figures, the stopping distance in feet from 60 mph and under load conditions with a light load and a maximum load. As an example, this changes for each motorcycle, naturally, due to weight and braking area. Yamaha's new TX 650 with a fully operational service brake under a light load will stop from 60 mph in 170 feet. With a maximum load, usually with a passenger, that would be 180 feet. The stopping distances will remain pretty much the same for most motorcycles. I have made a comparison of stopping distances of almost all of the major motorcycles and have determined that most of them are fairly consistent when figured from 60 mph. So, this information, although useful to you as to stopping distances, is not something you would want to consider in the purchasing of a new motorcycle.

For comparison's sake, I drive a 1973 Jaguar XJ 6 Sedan. It has 4-wheel disc brakes, considered to be the best brakes available. For comparison with the above motorcycle, the light-load stopping distance at 60 mph is 176 feet or 6 more feet than Yamahas TX 650. This changes with the maximum load though. With a passenger on the motorcycle, that maximum load changes to 180 feet, but the maximum with Jaguar drops to 159 feet. In other words, the increased load on the motorcycle lowered the safety factor and the increased load on the car increased it.

Acceleration and Passing Ability. This figure indicates the passing times and distances that can be met or exceeded by the vehicles to which it applies, in the situations outlined below. The low-speed pass assumes an initial speed of 20 mph and a limiting speed of 35 mph. The high-speed pass assumes an initial speed of 50 mph and a limiting speed of 80 mph.

What this means is, all motorcycle manufacturers have to use the same conditions on a low-speed pass; a truck moving 20 mph constant and a motorcycle is going to start passing him at 20 mph, but he can't go any more than 35 mph to pass him. What is the distance in feet and the time it takes to pass . . . that is, to pull out, pass, and get by and pull back in. This distance varies considerably, even among different motorcycles, yet it is important. It gives you an idea of the power of the motorcycle. As an example, the Kawasaki 1973 model S2 350cc makes a low-speed pass in 354 feet and 7.2 seconds. A Honda 1972 CL 350 makes the low-speed pass in 341 feet in 7 seconds, not much difference, less than 5 percent. In using the same two bikes as an example, the high-speed pass, which assumes you are passing a truck going a constant 50 mph and you enter your passing at 50 mph and your limiting speed is 80, will take the Kawasaki motorcycle 999 feet and 9.9 seconds to make the pass, and the Honda CL 350 takes 1165 feet and 12.4 seconds to pass. This gives you a clue as to the power of the motorcycle which indicates that it starts passing at 50 mph, it very quickly accelerates to 80 mph in order to pass— quicker than the CL 350. This tells you that the Kawasaki as opposed to the Honda in this particular model accelerates faster by 25 percent. Just for kicks, that same 73 Jaguar XJ 6 sedan makes a low-speed pass in 400 feet in 8.7 seconds, which is slower than both of the motorcycles in time and takes more distance. However, in the high-speed pass, the Jag takes 11.4 seconds and 1130 feet, less feet and less time in relation to the Honda, but the Kawasaki will take the Jag.

This information is vital to a consumer, and dealers complain that consumers are not reading it. What it means is, if you are trapped out on the turnpike and you have a passenger and you pull out to pass a vehicle, you want to be able to turn on the juice and pass and get back in. Anybody that drives a car knows the feeling of being trapped out in the passing lane unable to pass because of low power.

It is my suggestion that every person or consumer who buys a new motorcycle compare feature for feature one machine against another and especially some of the features relative to power. *A total number of "cc" is, in itself, not sufficient to give you an indication of total power.*

In general, you can't expect a 200cc machine with a rider or passenger to equal the passing ability of a 750cc bike, so you should look into Part 375 for whatever machine you intend to buy.

Braking is not really much of a problem with new motorcycles. They can all exceed most any car, but disc brakes are the newest innovation and they have a facility known to car buffs of being "fade-free." This is important to motorcyclists. Another feature of disc brakes is that they apparently work under adverse conditions such as rain and snow, and even wipe themselves fairly clean in muddy and sandy conditions. They always give you a constant pressure as opposed to the drum-type brakes, although they (drum) are very good when well sealed. They do get wet and, when they do, they have a tendency to "grab" which is not too dangerous in a 4-wheel vehicle but in a 2-wheel vehicle it can cause some skidding problems.

"Locking up" is a consideration with the leading-shoe-type brake, but very rarely are troubles experienced with a disc brake. Most brake troubles stem from poor maintenance anyway.

As I mentioned before, when and if you buy a used road motorcycle, try to stay as near to the current year as possible. More important, look for signs of "dumping." This would be scrapes at the handlebars, worn-off rubber grips, bangs or dents in the tank, bent fender, and so on. Dumping a woods bike is part of the game, and they are usually dumped at a low speed. The bikes themselves are built for this sort of treatment. Road bikes are built pretty ruggedly, but a spill or an accident can mean all kinds of trouble. Mechanics today can rebuild and repaint these machines so that they look as though they have never been cracked. I don't recommend them unless you know your dealer and, once again, we are back to that ole reliability feature. If the dealer stands behind his bike and it is a bargain—buy it. A funny thing about used motorcycles, they hold their trade-in value. Relatively speaking and working by percentages, you get a better deal trading in a used motorcycle than you do trading in a used car.

Check your tires for two things. One, for uneven wear. This should almost be an impossibility on a motorcycle, but it can happen. It shows that you are out of line. Make sure that you have at least 5mm of depth in the tread. In most modern tires you can tell when a tire is worn down when you hit the "cross block." About every three to four inches you will find rubber "barriers." These do not extend all the way across each rib on the front tire, but as the tire wears they come together. This indicates that the tire is worn even though there is tread there. On a car you might run a tire down a lot further, almost to no tread. Replace your tires long before the tread is down to

Modern motorcycle road tires are usually molded with the rib design in this photograph, and each incorporates what is known as a *wear indicator*. This particular tire, found on a Yamaha, is the one I consider the best from the point of view of "indication." As the tire wears down, the cross bars connect. At the time when they connect, the tire should be changed. As shown, it still has ⅛ inch or so of good thread in the center, but motorcycle tires generally don't last beyond 7000 miles. At least they shouldn't be used beyond that point.

the barrier. So, you aren't going to get as much mileage out of it. About 7000 or 8000 is all that I'll drive before I change tires! Look for cracks, abrasions, and other marks. Look along the rims to see where tire irons have been used to change tires. Tire irons are the only thing that should be used; screwdrivers are not tire irons. Very few motorcyclists buy irons, yet they should. If you do have to change a tire, you wreck a tire with a screwdriver or any other object. Flats can almost be prevented nowadays with special gook that can be blown into the tube at the time it is mounted, or any time, for that matter (see section maintenance). "Ping" each spoke to see that it is tight and the wheel is true.

You can tell a great deal about a used machine by the wear marks on the tanks and engine case where the rider's knees and boots have constantly rubbed the paint down. When the mileage is up there, at 10,000 miles you have a used bike, at 20,000 miles you have a really used bike, and at 40,000 miles you had better know what you are buying.

This is contrary to the same equivalent mileage in an automobile; at 10,000 a good car is just being broken in.

If you have any doubts about a machine, ask if you can have the name and address of the previous owner. Most dealers will give it to you and some dealers even put the previous owner's name on the tag and you can contact him.

I met a man who traded in a Norton the other day and with it went a little book. He had very carefully logged each oil change and each gas stop at every mileage, including the date and other pertinent information—for instance, whenever he had a flat tire or oiled the chain. Anybody buying that man's bike bought a gem. You knew everything about the bike for one thing, and the fact that he logged everything indicated to me that he was a man who was very careful about maintaining his bike, and, believe me, it was in top condition.

Every used bike, like every used car, is polished and put out on the line to look good. Taking it for a test run is fine, but be sure to check everything and I mean everything—right down to the chain, sprockets, and so on. Wiggle the rear sprocket to see if it is loose and look at the teeth to see if they have started to "hook," pull the chain away from the sprocket at the halfway point, and if it goes more than a half inch or you can see air through it, the chain is worn and/or the sprocket is worn. Ask the dealer to take the cover off the countershaft sprocket area and the ignition area and take the tank off. By looking under these three items you can tell a lot.

If the chain is worn, or the countershaft sprocket is worn, it will show with short peaks and you see wear areas. Taking the tank off and looking under it will tell you the condition of the coil and the wiring. If you find frayed and mashed wiring and a great deal of rust, make sure all the connections are tight and all the wiring is in good condition. Taking the cover off of the ignition area isn't going to tell you much, except that if it has been left out a lot the flywheel will be wet, perhaps rusty. Nothing serious, as long as everything runs in good order. Sure, you are going to see an accumulation of dirt and grease, but you will also be able to tell the approximate amount of wear and care that the bike has had.

Reputable dealers don't set back odometers. Some states have laws making setting an odometer back illegal.

Check the bottom of the safety bars to see if the bike has been scraped and, if it doesn't have safety bars, very carefully look the machine over in the daylight, and outdoors if possible.

Any modern motorcycle should start very easily. A kick or two should do it or three or four if it hasn't been used for a while. If the dealer has a lot of trouble starting a machine, be just a little bit wary. Out on the highway, if you are already an accomplished motorcyclist, check the suspension and look for high-speed wobbles. If the bike has a fairing on it, very carefully see if it is mounted securely before you drive and check the type of fairing. Some fairings raise the front end at 70 or 80 mph and she starts to hop like a rabbit. Check your tracking. This is best done on the center stand. Hold a piece of chalk or a pencil very close to the tire and spin the wheel in neutral. If you find over a 1/4-inch variance between the near and the far distance of the rim from the chalk on the tire, you may have an out-of-line wheel.

Check all control cables to see if they are stiff or if there is any corrosion on them or if there are broken strands protruding from either end. Look for wet spots around the cylinder to the case and "weeping" oil anywhere around the engine. If the engine is at all dirty, it should be cleaned and driven before you buy the bike. Oil drips and weeping will show instantly within just a few short miles after cleaning. Block the bike up and grab the front wheel at the axle and rock back and forth with the bike on the center stand. Clicking or looseness will tell you if your front fork bearings are in good shape or whether you have signs of wear.

The best way to check brakes on a used bike is to take the wheels off one by one. People don't usually do this, but they should. Look for abrasions in the front fork suspension seals. This will show up as leaking oil. Almost anywhere you see excessive oil or grease leaking, wipe it off or wash it off and trace it to its source.

On the road test of your secondhand machine, see that it goes into gear cleanly and positively. The shifting from gear to gear should be smooth and easy without "clunks." Place the bike on a center stand and eyeball the front and rear wheels to see that it's lined up. Check all chromium for nicks and scratches. There is a tremendous drop in power with a dirty muffler. Anything over 4000 miles has a dirty muffler. If it is cleaned out, it will run better, more smoothly, and give you more gas mileage. See that the throttle rolls on smoothly and has a spring return. You would be embarrassed to dump a bike and see it traveling on down the road causing much more severe damage than if you dumped with either a kill button or a return throttle spring.

One last thing: all imported and domestic-built motorcycles come with a "title," a certificate of ownership; in some states you cannot register the machine without one. Be sure and get the title if you buy your motorcycle from an individual. Banks usually keep these if the vehicle is mortgaged, so do not buy unless you have a clear title. And conversely, if you have finance, the bank will want the title.

2

What Must I Do to Maintain It?

As with any piece of machinery, cleanliness is next to godliness. Even a brand new motorcycle should be waxed as soon as you get it, and heavily. This doesn't mean just the chromium and painted parts, but the framework and bare metal, including aluminum cases. Be sure to wax the underside of the fenders as well as all hidden and difficult-to-get-at places where mud, salt, sand, and stones are going to hit. The wax serves many purposes—one is that it will keep the machine looking better and that is its cosmetic value. The other is the fact it will enable you to keep your machine cleaner and it protects the finish.

How often should you wash? This is more or less up to the amount of time you use it. If it is used in dry weather it isn't going to get too dirty, but if it is used during the rain or snow it will get dirty sooner and should be cleaned. Car washes are okay for washing motorcycles, but be careful to keep the hose out of the air cleaner box, wheel bearings, and your ignition (unless you have CDI, Condenser-Discharge-Ignition, commonly known as pointless ignition). The heavy detergent used in some car washes will not mar the finish so much as it will take off your coating of wax. It will cause irreparable harm if it gets into the air cleaner, and it may cause you a problem if it gets into your points and condenser area and wheel bearings.

Detergents from car washes will wash the grease out of your wheel bearings. When aiming the wand, be careful not to get inside the brake drums on leading-shoe-type brakes. This won't matter on discs. Repacking wheel bearings is quite a job and not recommended for light maintenance.

These are perhaps the only products that are mentioned in the book. I think they're important. The irons are the only thing to use for changing a tire. They are small, about 8 inches long, with one flat end and one curved end. Loctite has pretty well taken the place of cotter pins and lock washers and is generally carried in the toolbox of every motorcyclist. Vibration being a problem in cycling, a drop or two of Loctite is applied to every threaded bolt and prevents vibration from loosening the nuts. Dri Slide is about the only good lubrication for cables. The 2-ounce can shown is a bulk dispenser. Most cyclists have a small, hypodermic-needle type that they refill periodically. The applicator is much easier to use than the can. There are two types of chain lubes here—Chainmate and Beck/Arnley Chain Lube. Both foam under pressure, using a small-orifice applicator. I recommend these two highly. The biggest advantage is that they're not as messy as others and they do apply most of the lubrication to the chain. The engine degreaser is used prior to oiling the chain. It's a spray. After letting it sit for about five minutes, rinse it off with a water hose. LPS 1 is another motorcyclist's Most Important Product. It waterproofs all parts of your electrical system (see the text).

This might be just as good a place as any to point out that there is a fluid on the market called LPS I. This is a silicone-type spray, it is a magnificent insulator against water, and electricity is conducted through it. Take the cover off your ignition and spray freely, then it won't matter if you get a little water in it.

Talking about LPS, you might just as well spray your spark-plug leads as well as your diode bank. I regularly spray all around my battery, battery connections, condensers, diodes, electrical wiring, electrical connectors, fasteners, and the inside of the horn, which seems to be the recipient of a great deal of water and mud flung up by the wheel. Take off the headlamp cover and spray freely in there. Take off the Plexiglas taillight and the stoplight assembly cover and spray everything in there, including the base of each bulb and the socket connector. Wipe off the excess before you put everything back.

It is best to keep a good motorcycle inside a heated garage or shed. If it is left outside, even though it is covered, the moisture gets into it and it rusts. If you want to have easy starting, use the LPS as I mentioned above. Especially if you have to store your bike in a shed or outside for any length of time where humidity and moisture can get at it. Covering a bike only traps the moisture, but at least a cover will keep snow and other elements off it. Keep the gas tank as full as you possibly can to prevent condensation from forming on the inside walls of the tank.

Open the rubber sleeve connector between your air filter box and the throat of your carburetor and place a light coating of Vaseline on the inside of the throat just this side of the slide. This serves to trap minor particles of dirt that might get by the filter box. Grease and cover your battery cable connections and dress and trim all loose wiring. Wiring should be covered with rubber or plastic tubing and sealed on the ends so that dirt and moisture can't get into the cable carrier.

After you have ridden your bike approximately 100 miles, you should go over every nut and bolt and retighten. The tools that come with the machine should be sufficient for all of these projects. Admittedly, they are somewhat chintzy, but they are adequate for minor maintenance. Most motorcycle owners keep a separate set of tools back at the shop or garage or home with speed Allen wrenches with T handles, speed Phillips and straight drivers with T handles, ratchets and socket wrench sets in all of the common millimeter sizes.

The brake and clutch cable should be regularly oiled, usually with Dri Slide. It is a very messy graphite solution. However, they do have a small unit with a needle-type applicator for $1.95 that is ideal. You shake it until you get the ball rattling and with this "hypodermic needle" put a half a dozen drops at the cable connector at the handle, down the cable shielding. Do not put too much Dri Slide down the throttle control cable as this goes directly into the carburetor and can cause some uneven running and other problems. A good way to find out how much to put in it is to disconnect the cable of your front brake at the brake and apply Dri Slide to the handle end until you see it come out the other end—say, four or five heavy drops. Wait a while in between each drop. If it appears at the fourth, fifth, or sixth, whatever, subtract two and this is the number of drops you put down the throttle cable and you will know it won't go into the carburetor.

Check your forks for oil leaks regularly; especially check your chrome tubes for pits. If you have a really good road bike you will find that your fork tubes are covered with accordion rubbers. These things have a tiny air hole at the back or the inside with a radiator hose clamp. Whenever you travel in wet weather for extended periods of time, you will have to loosen these and let the water out. I don't know how it gets in there, but it does.

If you have a chain machine, you are going to have to adjust that chain constantly and you are going to have to see that it is oiled properly all of the time. Although the gallon can is the best and most economical way to buy oil, I still like the aerosol cans even though they are far more expensive. They seem to be less messy and easier and quicker to apply. Such as Beck Arnley's Chain Lube. Remember that each time you adjust the chain you have to adjust the rear brake.

Chain-driven motorcycles need constant adjustment, especially when they are new, and constant oiling. It is a chore, but break yourself in and start oiling. Start forming a good habit of adjusting your chain regularly. Sit on the saddle, then feel the chain on the lower strand halfway between the two sprockets. There should be no more than three-quarters of an inch play up and down with you in the saddle.

Testing for chain tightness requires that the chain be no looser than ¾ to 1 inch, and it is tested sitting in the saddle. Reach over with your left hand and pull the bottom, not the top, length of chain up to you. If the distance from this pull to slack is over 1 inch, readjust your chain. Sorry to use a woods bike in this picture, but most road bikes have a muffler going by this point and, although you can check the chain behind the muffler, you can't see it in the photograph.

After a while you will learn which wrench goes to which nut and if you get into the practice of using the tool kit that comes with the bike, you will always have the right wrench handy.

I throw away all cotter pins on axle bolts and wherever else they are on the bike and put in aircraft brass safety wire. I also carry a little roll of it in my tool bag. It is very soft brass and you can put it in the same hole that the cotter pin goes in and twist it quickly with a pair of pliers and clip off the ends.

After a long trip or anytime that I have gone over some rough roads, I take a wrench and "ping" my spokes; this is a check for tightening. They will give you back a musical sound. If you hear a dull "thud," you know you have a dead spoke and also a bent rim.

As soon as you get your machine and you are home some night, put it up on the center stand and take off the rear wheel. Look at the brake shoe and the sprocket and drum and how the whole thing is put together. The instructions are in the book that comes with the bike. Put the rear wheel back together again and do the same thing for the front wheel.

Wherever disc brakes are included on a new motorcycle, the brake fluid level must be constantly checked. Disc brakes do not need any maintenance other than this single check. On the rare occasion that you find the brake fluid decreasing rapidly, check for leaks.

Ordinary greasing and oiling is a standard procedure and the times to do the different positions are usually listed in the instruction book. The manufacturers have been very thorough in writing good instruction books. I find that the Japanese are better than the German or the English.

Even though a rider might not be mechanically inclined, psychologically it is very good for his confidence and his ego to do as much maintenance as he can on his own bike. The more you do, the more you have confidence in your own ability and in the bike's ability. All maintenance is a nuisance. Almost everyone wants to ride, but in a recent survey of dealers, I asked the question: "What is the single biggest problem you find with motorcycles that have been traded in?" Almost 100 percent answered that the machines were all generally run down in every department. Poor maintenance had caused this condition. When I started the research for this book, I had anticipated wornout rings or abuse of the engine in some way, but I had not realized that *poor maintenance has been the cause of almost 100 percent of all motorcycle problems.*

In many ways, a motorcycle is like an airplane. Your life may depend on keeping it in good condition and this is more so than with a car. As an added safety feature, a pilot is required to make certain checklists both before he takes off and before he even leaves the ramp area. In examining instruction books for this book, I have found that without an exception, each instruction book had a "Check Point Periodic Inspection Guide." If this checklist were followed religiously, before a ride other than going to the store or on errands, I am sure a motorcycle would last many thousands of miles.

Some machines such as BMW have been known to go over

100,000 miles and I personally know of two such bikes. Obviously, these were taken care of. Make up your own checklist, encase it in a plastic envelope, and attach it under your seat. Run through it constantly.

Learn how to adjust the clutch and adjust the two different brakes. Constantly check the nuts and nut tightening.

Battery problems almost all occur from overfilling. The connections should be kept clean, tight, and well greased— preferably covered with rubber insulator.

The carburetor can be adjusted usually in about two areas. The Idle Mixture and the Engine Idle Speed Throttle Cable—I don't recommend fooling beyond these unless you have some experience.

Changing the oil is a messy project. It should be done after the engine is warmed up. Some machines have one and some two oil drain bolts on the bottom. After draining out the oil, return the drain bolts, tighten up, add the proper amount of oil to the tank, warm up the engine again, stop it and check the oil level, then bring it up to the proper position.

Air filters are usually equipped with reusable oil-impregnated foam air filters. These should be removed and cleaned at least once a month and more often if the motorcyclist has been riding on dirt roads. They should be cleaned and gasolined, squeezed out, blown dry, and a light sprinkling of Filtron Filter Oil sprayed on, and the filter returned. Don't put so much oil on the filter that it drips, and *never, never under any circumstance run the motorcycle without the air filter*. Two things, dirt and dust, will be able to pass right into the cylinder and this will cause all kinds of engine problems. More air will flow to the engine and there won't be enough gasoline for all of the air. This lean mixture will cause higher engine temperatures and possibly damage your engine.

As for ignition timing and tappet clearance, it is not that much of a job and I really think a good motorcyclist should learn to do these two service checks. The tools required are very simple, and if you go to your dealer I am positive he will teach you how to use them. If you are learning to *time*, you can learn to adjust and replace your own breaker points since the ignition timing changes when the points are replaced. If you have CDI, Condensor-Discharge-Ignition, commonly known as electronic ignition or "pointless" ignition, you won't have this problem. It is far more reliable—yet in many thousands of miles of driving bikes over the past forty years, I have had very few "point" problems.

The spark plug is very much like a thermometer. The way it looks on the bottom will tell you if the engine is operating correctly. If your plug and your machine are in good working order, that white insulator on the bottom will have a light tan color or a "cherry"-looking color and be dry. If it is dark brown or black you are running rich and you need a plug with a hotter heat range. Look on the porcelain tip and if it is actually white or the electrodes start to melt, then you need a plug with a colder heat range and you are running too lean. It won't do any good to experiment with different heat range spark plugs. Even many mechanics don't know which way it should go and you can't tell if it is the spark plug that is actually at fault. It is okay to replace a standard plug with a duplicate plug of the same manufacturer.

Even when you replace a plug, be sure you always clean the gasket surface and use a new gasket. Make it a rule not to

Notice the two spark plugs. One is oily, black, and sooty; the other has a dry clean look. If this picture were in color, the clean one would be light tan and brown. The other is what we call fouled. This is common in many bikes for the first 300 or 400 miles and not that serious. It could be caused by poor carburetion or poor oil mixture. The correct plug is the tan one, and this is what it should look like.

wrench them in, but put them in with your fingers; tighten with a wrench. As long as you have that LPS I handy, why don't you spray a little on the threads so the plug will go in easier? Gapping is something you should do. A wire feeler gauge usually somewhere between .020 and .024 is the proper gap for most machines.

Changing fork oil every 3000 miles in standard on most machines. There are two little Phillips head screws at the bottom of the forks, usually on the outside. By taking these out and compressing the forks several times to pump all the remaining oil out, you will clear it. Reinsert your drain screws and make sure they are tight and remove the fork cap that is on the top of each fork tube. These are the great big hex nuts. There are usually somewhere between 150 and 200cc of oil in each fork leg. Make sure that you put the same amount in each tube. I suggest you replace with automatic transmission fluid "F." I have tried every fork lubrication material on the market, all of which are quite expensive, and for what it's worth I find ATF still the best and also the cheapest. The qualities that are needed in a fork oil are nonfoaming and its ability to retain its viscosity at extreme temperatures.

Transmission oils on those bikes that require it should be changed approximately every 3000 miles. Shaft-driven motorcycles have a Rear Wheel Drive Oil level as well that must be changed and checked along with the Drive Shaft Housing Oil Level.

Tire pressure is one of the single most important maintenance features on any motorcycle and it should be kept fairly constant. Normally the front carries less pressure than the rear because of weight distribution. The average runs around 23 pounds in the front and 25 pounds in the rear. I especially like to keep my tire pressures up in rain.

I have left tire changing to the last. It is a messy job, difficult, and it requires a "knack." *A screwdriver is not a tire iron.* Much damage has been done to tires and tire rims and wheels by screwdrivers used as tire irons. If your motorcycle tool kit does not come with tire irons, may I suggest that you buy a pair because you are definitely going to need them. Another item that might be helpful with tires is one of the new liquid emulsions placed inside the tube. One of the best is known as "Flat-Proof." About 4 to 8 ounces of this fluid is placed in each tire. Buy it at the time you buy your motorcycle. The material effectively seals nail holes and the like. Most motorcycle tool kits come with a tube repair kit but, if yours doesn't, buy one. You might need it.

The newer and larger motorcycles are getting very sophisticated with special starting motors and 3-phase alternators, both of which require the services of a trained mechanic. Diodes are used for rectification, and the old-fashioned voltage regulator has now been replaced with the diodes and the mechanical contactor. These are beyond the average rider.

Centrifugal timing advance mechanisms advance the spark timing as speed increases. This mechanism is new on motorcycles and you won't have much trouble with it. The effect of its being out of balance would be excessive vibration and rough, uneven running. It requires an adjustment that your dealer should make.

3

Accessories and
Other Gingerbread

I CLASSIFY accessories for the road machine in two groups: those that I consider essential and those I consider frills. This is subject to each man's personal needs and likes and dislikes but I won't equivocate in regard to the first two items. One is the safety bars, formerly known as "crash bars." In forty years of riding I have been dumped or dumped purposely and have had accidents and have driven military motorcycles and *I believe in the safety bars.* I believe they save the driver's legs when he goes down. I don't like to start off a chapter with a negative attitude, but I do believe in preventative safety and I believe these bars can and do save extensive personal damage.

Most of my road machines in the past fifteen years have been BMWs and these have two horizontally opposed cylinders

A Holsclaw trailer will hold three bikes or two or one. One of the better makes and very popular with the bigger bikes.

The BMW stripped and chromed. This isn't a Chopper, but it's a very pretty-looking bike. Note the chromed electrics cover and the chrome exhaust covers.

"sticking out from the sides of the engine." I can remember one event very vividly; I was leaving a friend's house one January in New England where I live, and as I rounded a corner of a country road, I ran into an area of "black ice." I couldn't see it because it was night. Since I ride most of the winter and in the spring and fall but not at all in July and August, I have long since become accustomed to driving in the cold and, in the winter, in snow, ice, and rain. In this particular case, I was on to the ice at a slow speed before I could take any corrective action. So, I danced across this black ice like a wounded ballerina, and down I went at about 20 mph and promptly skidded for 40 or 50 feet. I was thankful that at least there were no bare spots that would stop the machine. The combination of the safety bars and the horizontal cylinders

A dressed-up BMW. Note the painted black cylinders with chrome trim. Also the chromium heat shields on the exhaust as well as chromed electrics cover.

saved my leg, and since I wear very heavy protective clothing, which I will go into another chapter, I wasn't hurt. My pride was bruised more than anything else, although the next day I did wake up with a black and blue mark on my left hip. I picked my machine up at the end of the ice and started it with the electric starter and took off. The next day I examined the machine and found to my distinct pleasure that the bars were not damaged but I did notice that the rocker cover was worn almost through. Those cylinders had once again taken the brunt of the shock. This is why I always consider the BMW one of the safest of all the road bikes.

The second accessory engenders a lot of controversy. This is the business of windshields and fairings vs. none.

For some unknown reason it seems to be the notion of the

Notice the Mickey Mouse horn, which should be substituted for a good pair of either air horns or Hellas, and two sets of crash bars. One set of these roll bars is for the bike and another set to protect the liquid-cooling system. Excellent protection for both rider and bike on a Suzuki.

youngest of the road riders that to give in and put a windshield or a fairing on their bike is to sissify them or identify them with the older rider. There is probably some truth in that, but anybody who does any sort of touring at all other than local to and from work is going to have to give in eventually and get himself a windshield or a fairing.

Riding without these subjects you to an unbelievable amount of buffeting, and over a long period of time it can destroy the stamina of even the strongest of men. In the summer the average motorcyclist rides into literally hundreds upon hundreds of insects. Just look at his jacket. His face shield, if he doesn't have a windshield, is covered with bloodied debris from the night fliers. If he is a real purist and insists on no helmet, you can tell he is a real dyed-in-the-wool outdoor motorcyclist by the bugs in his teeth!

Such foolhardiness simply doesn't make good sense. To those who do long-distance touring, I don't think I even have to sell the idea, but for those who are embarking on their first trips away from home, you will find your comfort tremendously increased with a windshield. For one thing, you will be warmer, and most windshields can be taken off for summertime driving. In long-distance touring they are needed even on the hottest of summer days. If you run into rainstorms, a windshield is an excellent buffer from a comfort point of view and it enables you to keep dry and to maintain your ability to drive in the rain. A windshield properly installed and properly anchored should be one inch below the driver's eyes. The force of the wind will blow rain or snow a few inches above the windshield, clearing his eyes, yet the rider will be able to see without looking through the windshield.

Nowadays, fairings are more popular—Bates, Wixom, Vetter, Flanders, and Avon and Kulan are a few. Two of these fairings are attached to the frame of the bike, with the headlights inside the fairing. This means that when you go around a corner, the fairing follows the main frame, and the steering mechanism turns independently inside the fairing. A little

>

A BMW with a Windjammer fairing. Note a number of things. Outboard directional signals, twin air horns, the best chrome bar with outrigger, quartz-halogen power lights for night driving, crash bar protection for bike and rider, folding chrome foot pegs on crash bar for long-distance change of position.

Note crash guard on 4-cylinder Honda, built-in directional signals in fairing and the use of rubber handlebar grips as foot rests in two positions on crash bar. Note backrest attached to luggage rack, for passenger.

hairy experience, but those who have them claim they are very happy with them. Other fairings attach to the handlebars.

Fairings must be very carefully mounted and balanced. A poorly mounted fairing can cause a high-speed wobble. The fairings named above have been designed with the help of air tunnels to determine whether or not the airflow would cause the front wheel to hop. Properly mounted according to manufacturer's recommendations, these fairings are well designed.

The Avon and Vetter fairings cost considerably more than the others because of the larger design and greater protection and the headlight that is included.

There is an esthetic problem in this business of fairings and you begin to wonder whether you are riding a motorcycle anymore with configuration so changed. The handling characteristics change as well, and some of the original pleasures derived from motorcycling seem to be submerged in the propelling of a projectile.

There is no doubt about it, fairings offer warmth, protection, and a great deal of comfort from the elements. Try to ride

A Vetter Windjammer fairing which is bolted to the frame of the bike. The handlebars turn inside the fairing. The headlight is attached to the fairing. This is a right turn using that fairing. The headlight is visible from in front.

A Vetter Windjammer fairing bolted to the frame of the bike. Handlebars shown turn to the left to illustrate that the fairing stays stationary. Two pouch pockets, one on right and one on left, hold a great deal of miscellaneous junk.

the machine with one on and again with one off. You will notice the difference. The new BMW R90S comes with a racing-type fairing built onto the motorcycle. This may be the beginning of a trend.

The luggage rack is another accessory that you will buy sooner or later. It is the forerunner to the saddlebag. They come in all kinds of shapes and sizes, usually chrome, and some black. The purchase of a couple of "bungee" rubber ties makes it comparatively easy to tie down rain suits, coats, sleeping bags, and so on, for those who wish to use a bike for touring. It is almost a "must" for anybody traveling any distance, since you cannot foretell what kind of weather you might run into or what kind of clothes you might need. Some people attach all sorts of boxes on the rack, some are made of fiber glass that matches the saddlebags; these are known as panniers. You can buy a simple chrome rack for about $10 or go all the way to $100 for the hand-painted fiber-glass pannier ice chest with combination locks.

Packing all sorts of equipment on the rear of the motorcycle seems natural, and it is a common practice. However, I do wish motorcyclists would think before they do such a thing,

Here is a typical luggage rack in chromium, almost a must. Since most luggage racks stick way out to the rear, don't overload it. That could cause bike to be off balance. The luggage rack when loaded could very easily hide the taillight. Another no-no.

primarily because such a practice causes the bike to be out of balance. The weight on the rear causes a change in the handling characteristics of the bike. Anything added onto the bike other than the rider and a passenger changes these characteristics. Engineering geometry of a motorcycle includes the possible use of a passenger and/or saddlebags or luggage racks, but *excessive* weight applied to the rear of a motorcycle causes front-wheel "wobble," a hopping condition. Add a passenger and you have an unsafe condition, especially if you run into inclement weather.

Overloaded to the rear. The rider could experience a high-speed wobble and loss of control due to the fact that all of the weight is put aft of the rear wheel. If he's riding with a passenger, he's really looking for trouble.

Long-distance touring does require a lot of luggage and equipment, but it must be very carefully packed and distributed so that the weight is equal, front and rear. The area between the handlebars will carry quite a lot of well-packed supplies. More if there is a windshield or fairing on the bike. Whatever you pack anywhere on the bike, it must be balanced side to side and really secured from buffeting and high-speed wind damage. Cruising 70 mph is a 70 mph wind picking at your ties.

Saddlebags come in many styles, the most modern of them are made of fiber glass with demountable lids. Even those that are manufactured for a specific bike are not as good as some of the others. You must determine whether they affect the

Overloaded on the rear. If he's riding with a passenger he could experience instability in the front end and front-wheel wobble. Note umbrella aft of taillight. Incidentally taillight is hidden.

This is the rear end of a full-dressed Harley. Beautiful crash guards, warning lights, taillights, and suitcase panniers. Note the deluxe stereo deck between the handlebars up forward, and the wide footrests instead of pegs.

geometry of the machine and cause front-wheel wobble. The best types are those that allow little or no air between them and the rear wheel. Those that stick out leaving space for an airfoil cause greatest problems whether they are square, round, teardrop shape, or what. They should be well fitted, in close to the wheel. Even this is no guarantee of a good bag. Check for hardware. Some of the lids blow off because of insecure fastenings. Everything that is put into a saddlebag should be wrapped in polyethylene or polyurethane bags. This is a seal against moisture. Wind and rain do get inside saddlebags and can wreak havoc with your personal belongings.

Cameras should not, I repeat! should not, be carried in the saddlebag unless they are heavily insulated from vibration with foam rubber. One of the biggest problems camera repair people have is the loosening of small internal screws in a camera. If you must carry a camera, sling it around your shoulder. Your body will act as a dampener. If you are determined to put it in a saddlebag, wrap it in cloth so that it doesn't vibrate.

Everything you put on your luggage rack should be wrapped in plastic bags for protection against inclement weather. Make sure all flaps are sealed and all folds are to the rear.

It goes without saying that you should pack the things you need most on top. A good pair of saddlebags on one of those reasonably large machines will pack a considerable amount of material, as much as a couple of medium-size suitcases. Considering you have those plus a luggage rack area, you can carry

There are a number of interesting things about this picture. Note the large saddlebags. These should be lined with foam rubber. They are good bags in that they also include warning lights. The seat rail is for the passenger to hang onto, a no-no, for balance would be too far back. Note the directional signals, large and spaced out so they are not confused with the taillight.

A thermos ice chest on the back of this bike is an invitation to disaster. The two saddlebags are properly attached to the bike. A problem could develop with this type of bag if the lid-locking mechanism is inadequate.

an awful lot. Obviously, careful consideration should be given as to how the bags are packed so that the weight is evenly distributed.

Sissy bars on the end of a luggage rack serve a practical purpose in that you can wrap a blanket or a sleeping bag around them and they serve as a backrest for the rear passenger. With all your weight in the rear of your motorcycle, it can cause problems as mentioned above. So, wherever possible, start adding on the front.

All states have laws forbidding high-powered quartz-iodide lights in this country, and I feel this is a shame. They are very powerful beam lights, and they are outlawed because they are so bright that they have a tendency to blind an oncoming driver. I don't like to write a book and suggest anybody break a law, but may I suggest that you replace your headlamp with a quartz halogen or quartz-iodide-type seal-beam headlight,

Another type of saddlebag, hand-painted and with a good lid latch. Attaching hardware looks Mickey Mouse. Make sure you buy the set that fits properly.

Note sissy bar with backrest for passenger, plus crash-bar protection for saddlebags, and hand painting enhancing overall appearance.

making absolutely certain that your power system will carry it, and at the same time check one lamp against the other to make absolutely certain that you have over *500 feet* of forward visibility. If you feel that you do not want to fool with the headlight configuration, maybe you would be able to mount one of these quartz-iodide units on your safety bars. Aim these so that they are in a low profile, but they are vitally necessary, especially for black night driving.

A motorcyclist riding at night has better night vision than an automobile driver. He can "see more." Primarily because he is not disturbed by the peripheral or ambient light inside a car. His only consideration is whatever miniature dash lights he has on his motorcycle. Consequently, the pupils of his eyes will dilate somewhat more, enabling him to have better vision.

A motorcyclist must be constantly alert because of miscellaneous objects in the road (see Night Driving), so an accessory light may be quite useful.

First note the crash bar. This could save your leg in the event of a spill. It also serves as a hanger for a special pair of high-powered quartz-halogen lights. These are illegal for running, but they're great for emergency and for those superdark roads at night. On 4-cylinder Honda.

Close-up of air horns, crash bar, and Windjammer fairing with quartz-halogen lights, mounted in the fairing.

Other accessories, which some may consider gingerbread and some may consider essential, are alarm systems. There are usually two different types of these systems. One has a radio transmitter and receiver. The rider carries the receiver with him when he goes inside to warm up or quench his thirst, so that if someone tampers with the machine it "beeps" and he has an opportunity to run out and apprehend the tamperer. The other system starts a loud screeching noise that serves to scare the culprit and at the same time warn the owner that the bike is being tampered with.

Heavy chains encased in plastic so they don't scratch the paint, plus bars that go through wheels, are quite successful as antitheft devices. Most modern bikes also have fork locks that prevent the bike from being steered so it must be picked up and carried away. Gas tank locks are common as are seat and helmet locks and toolbox locks. Saddlebags also come with locks, but most of these locks are very inadequate and are more or less to deter the casual vandal rather than the serious thief.

This license plate holder is in reality a "cycle alarm." Anyone tampering with this bike will set off a loud howling alarm. A very good device.

Probably one of the most inexpensive of all accessories is a second mirror for the right-hand handlebar. Any serious rider will put one on. People do creep up on your right.

A leg splash guard can be made for most bikes from a little piece of aluminum and some rubber from an inner tube. You don't really appreciate these until you are driving through a series of puddles after a rainstorm; usually you're soaked from the splashing of the front wheel.

Leg guards are manufactured by Enduro Products Inc. of Milford, Connecticut. They also make a very sophisticated line of saddlebags of fiber glass for most large touring bikes. Their leg guards are there to protect you, not so much from rain, but from the cold. These are used by the "all year around" riding buffs in the Northeast and Northwest and North Middle West. If you have ever gone on a long trip and wound up with a cold knee, you would appreciate these.

Tank pouches have recently become popular. These are little zippered vinyl or leather pouches with an acetate cover for sliding in a full road map, and they open up so you can carry a few personal belongings. Cigarette lighters, radios, even tape decks are possible accessories. Some people will put

50

A heavy duty chain with lock. A must if you wish to have your bike when you come out from having a bite to eat.

Another fairing with a pannier and backrest well designed, but it could cause a problem with weight so far back of the rear axle.

Sissy bar with backrest and high luggage rack so as not to obscure large taillights. Probably the best taillight assembly made in 1973. Note double mirrors; a must for a good motorcycle.

AM-FM radio with tape deck on full-dressed Harley. Note triangular chrome strips either side of windshield for face protection.

Note the twin speakers for a radio, a compass, a cigarette lighter on the right fork assembly, a home away from home.

Another AM-FM radio with tape deck on a full-dressed Harley. These Motorola units are very popular and they do make driving a little more comfortable. But you need a very superior electric system. So far, I recommend this only on a Harley.

Well-designed bags fitted close in to the bike prevent airflow from upsetting geometry. Backrest attached to pannier on luggage rack makes a practical use of the space.

on an unbelievable amount of accessories. I am not knocking it
—each to his own. People who travel all over the world on
motorcycles, and some do, have special requirements and have
learned what the requirements are during the trip. The mountain climber and the desert rider have other considerations.
You can easily see the need for thermos bottles, drinking water
containers, extra gas can, and all sorts of camping, cooking,
sleeping, and wearing attire.

One last item I would like to discuss is the addition of a
horn. All modern motorcycles come with a horn. I don't think
any of them are adequate and, since it is a pet peeve, I am
going to take the writer's prerogative and elaborate on my
theory. Years ago, when motorcycles were not as common as
they are now, one of the cyclist's biggest problems was animals.
Dogs in particular. Dogs would run out in the streets barking
and snarling at a motorcycle. Two or three things would happen—once in a while the driver or rider would panic and
swerve and endanger himself due to oncoming traffic or perhaps lose his balance or weave in such a way that he would hit
an oil slick or sandy spot. Many riders have kicked out at dogs,
which throws them off balance. Dogs have misjudged their
speed and actually run into motorcycles and an object as big as
a medium-to-large-size dog can throw a bike, causing a spill
with damage to the rider and motorcycle.

In 1966, I owned a BMW R69S. I happened to buy a pair
of Hella chromium-plated horns and the first thing I noticed
was that, whenever a dog came out after me and I pressed those
powerful horns, he stopped dead in his tracks and he actually
had a look of puzzlement. I deduced that one of two things had
happened. One is that either the resonance or the frequency of
the sound of those horns confused his instinct or training or
the horns were reminiscent of a large automobile and he be-
came frightened. This happened more than once. Since then, I
have never had trouble with animals with this type of horn.

The second reason for buying a big set of horns has to do
with "defensive driving" which will be covered in another
chapter. Psychologically, a driver of a car is looking for quick
subconscious impressions of a large vehicle 18 to 20 feet in a
boxlike rectangular shape so when he pulls out of a driveway
or side street he will completely ignore "the image of a motorcycle and rider." It simply doesn't register on his brain, and

Note the very large taillight assembly and the position of the directional signals. Also the side reflectors. All of these devices enhance your visibility to the other driver.

this fundamental premise is accepted by almost all serious motorcyclists. Since it does exist, there must be some way to call attention to the motorist that there is something that he should take into consideration when he makes a decision as to pulling out, passing, and so on. I find that liberal use of these large horns triggers his subconscious into his conscious and he takes notice of me. In any event, it does work. If you are buying a machine or you already own one, please investigate this type of horn.

So there is an endless array of accessories that can be included on a motorcycle. Everyone personalizes his own bike. The need for individuality is prevalent among all humans, and there are many accessories that mean nothing to one person and a great deal to another. In this chapter I have tried to name those that I feel worthy of mention. I use brand names only when I feel it is important.

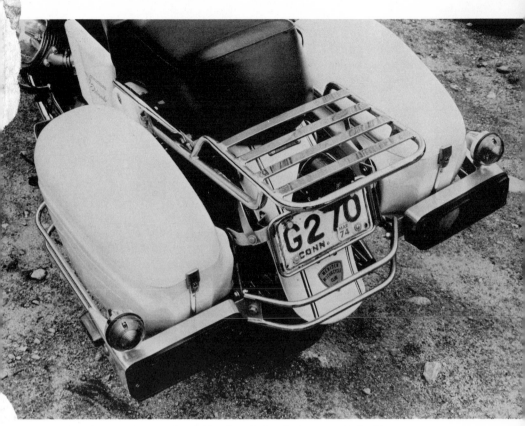

Notice the very large pair of directional signals incorporated with a warning light, and the directional signals far out. Directional signals are always yellow and should be mounted as far away from the taillight as possible. Here again, the luggage rack has a tendency to hide the spotlight.

4

How Do I Learn to Ride?

The habits formed by the beginning rider will carry throughout his riding career. For this reason, it is most important that the course or outline developed for teaching motorcycle riding be clear, concise, and well coordinated. For the purpose of this section of the book, it is assumed that the novice already knows how to ride a bicycle. For that rare person who might buy a motorcycle without having ever ridden a bicycle, he or she had best start by riding one.

It is not a very good idea to learn to ride on someone else's motorcycle. I am also going to assume here that the reader has bought either a secondhand machine or a new one and wishes to learn to ride it well. There are some things about a motorcycle that are pretty standard. The location of the controls is the same on all motorcycles with the exception of one or two special-purpose bikes such as the Bultaco, which is primarily a competition bike.

The only road bikes mentioned in this book whose shifting mechanism is on the right side of the machines are the Triumph, BSA, and the Norton, which are all British. All of the others have the shifting mechanism on the left and are shifted by the left toe or foot.

Your first approach to learning how to ride will be to read the instruction book. It is best to read the instruction book with someone who knows how to ride, since he can point out the various controls and go over each one with you. The section pertaining to location of the controls in the instruction book is usually in the first section. While reading the instruction book, place the motorcycle on the center stand and sit on it with the key off. First determine the key positions. These are very similar to those in your automobile. Next check and memorize your gas petcock switch position. This lever usually has three positions on motorcycles: On, Off, and Reserve. Put it in the Off position, but memorize the On position and the Reserve position.

For the first hour, you are going to work with the following controls and the following controls only:

Right Front Brake. Attached to your right handlebar, pulling in lever brakes the front wheel. Also actuates rear brake light.

Throttle. Also on your right handlebar—it is the movable rubber handgrip (takes the place of the foot accelerator in your car).

Clutch Lever. On the left handlebar. Pulling it in disengages the clutch, and letting it out engages the clutch. Notice at this time that the left handlebar grip does not move. It is glued on.

Rear Brake Lever. Your right foot actuates this. There should be about an inch play so that your foot can touch the lever without actually pushing it. The ball of your foot and the heel rest on the peg and the *Rear Brake Lever* is actuated by the toe of your right foot. The ball or heel of your foot and the peg are acting as a hinge, enabling you to give a smooth application of the rear brake. Under *no* circumstances is the heel or foot to be off the peg when using this brake or you will be "stabbing" at the brake. Stabbing will cause uneven application and could cause lockup and skidding. This movement also actuates the rear brake light.

Beginning instruction starts with knowing the location of various parts of the motorcycle. Most of this should have been learned by the prospective student from reading the instruction book prior to the time with the instructor. Here my gal Friday is familiarizing herself with various parts of the motorcycle being pointed out by the instructor.

Most young people started out in automatic cars, so they're not used to shifting for each gear. The use of the clutch is something new to many people who have driven automatics only. Here, George is pointing out the use of the clutch.

Gearshift Lever. Actuated by the left foot. Here, too, the ball and heel rest on the left peg, which acts as a hinge. However, there is a difference in the action of the toe. Most motorcycles shift "One Down," so the shift lever must be pushed once down to get into first gear, then up, with the top of the toe gently pushing it up into neutral. Pushing it up once again brings it into second gear and again into third, and again into fourth and again into fifth. This is assuming there are five gears on your bike; for six gears, shift up once more. All motorcycles are fairly standard in this category—one down, four or five up. Each shift is accompanied by a corresponding engaging and disengaging of the clutch lever.

Now basically, those are your driving controls. Other controls such as your horn, lights, and positions of other things on your motorcycle will not be discussed in this chapter. We are concerned primarily with the following:

1. Right Front Brake (Right Handlebar)
2. Throttle Control (Right Handlebar)
3. Clutch Lever (Left Handlebar)
4. Right Rear Brake (Right-foot Actuated)
5. Gearshift Lever (Left-foot Actuated)

These five are our driving controls. Sitting on the motorcycle and memorizing each one and learning the coordination between your hand and your brain and foot, go through a drill. The drill should be done in the following manner and in first gear only without the engine running:

1. Pull the clutch lever in
2. Push the shift lever down
3. Slowly let out the clutch handle
4. Increase the throttle slowly
5. Moving forward in first gear only, clutch out, throttle on
6. Roll off the throttle back to idle
7. Pull in clutch lever
8. "Toe" shift lever back to neutral
9. Slow bike down with rear brake lever
10. Add front brake as needed

The instructor uses a checklist and a prescribed pattern to see that she follows each part of chapter 4. At the present, he's pointing out the shift level. She is to practice shifting back and forth on the stand.

That is the *Primary Drill* and it should be carried out from memory on the motorcycle without the engine running. After it is memorized and thoroughly memorized, it is time to start the motorcycle—still on the center stand. Before you turn the key, make sure that the gearshift is actually in neutral. It is easy to shift when a motorcycle is rolling. When it is stationary it will sometimes lock up in gear and you might have to get off the motorcycle and spin the rear wheel with your hand to disengage the gearshift mechanism. After you have determined neutral (the wheels spin free with the clutch lever released), go back to your instruction book and practice starting the motorcycle with the kick lever. This is a knack, a special skill. It is easy once it is learned, but it can be frustrating and difficult. Most good motorcycles should start in no more than two or three kicks. The start sequence is as follows:

1. Turn gas tank lever to "On"
2. Turn switch to "On"
3. Kick starting lever sharply
4. Simultaneously add a touch of throttle on the end of the downstroke

Your motorcycle should start. If it doesn't, either your kick wasn't sharp enough or your engine was cold and needed a "tickle." On most motorcycles there is either a choke lever or there is a button attached to the carburetor that may be pushed to give a shot of "prime." Try a shot of prime and rekick. Once the engine is running, allow it time to smooth out. Often putting a motorcycle into gear and letting the clutch out with a cold motorcycle will cause it to stall. You may think it is your "not so smooth technique of shifting," whereas in fact it could just be a cold engine.

Once the engine is warm, assuming you are sitting on the motorcycle and it is on the center stand, go through your first 1–10 First Gear or "Primary" Drill. Do the practice of your front and rear braking even though you are not moving. Go through this drill at least 10 times with the engine running on a center stand and you in the saddle.

The next procedure will be to practice this off the center stand in a large paved area, such as a schoolyard or parking lot, but make sure this is done only under supervision of your instructor, since he is going to be responsible for traffic in the area, and you are going to be concentrating on driving. Make your first runs straight ahead. Your objective is to start your motorcycle, put it in first as per your 1–10 drill and move forward, take it out of gear, and come to a stop. This should be done a minimum of 10 times. At the end of 10 times you are going to do 5 more drills, 1–10 except that, instead of shifting out of gear as per number 8, you are going to leave it in gear and hold the clutch in with the clutch lever when you come to a stop. This means you are still in gear. With your right foot on the ground and your left hand holding the clutch in, you will place it in neutral. Do 10 more drills of 1–10 with this added requirement. You will notice the difficulty that will stay with you as long as you are a motorcyclist and that is to "find neutral." Most modern road machines have a "green light" that shows up on your dash and this is something you will look for. It tells you where neutral is. Do not rely on your own judgment of "feel." It simply isn't that reliable. Up to this point, you have made 30 maneuvers. Ten, going through the drill on your center stand static. Ten, moving under power on a straight line disengaging the shift mechanism. Ten, leaving the shift mechanism in gear and just pulling the clutch in.

At this point you should do more or less practice depending on the degree of your learning speed. If you feel competent, now is the time to go through the drill doing 10 more, only as you get up to number 8 you change and pull in your clutch lever and with your left foot shift up to second gear past neutral and then repeat the rest of the first drill up to coming to a stop. At this point, you can either come to a stop with the gear shift in position or back to neutral. My suggestion is to leave it in gear and come to a stop. This should then be practiced until it is mastered.

At the end of this time you have now done 40 different drills and it shouldn't have taken you over an hour and it is time for a turn. Go back to drill 1–10, and your instructor will set up a wide sweeping turn for you. It should be an 180° turn (half circle). I don't suggest a full circle yet. The turn should be practiced 180° to the left and to the right. All done in first gear and all coming to a stop in gear with the clutch in. Ten of these should be done to the left and 10 to the right, and they should not be done consecutively, but alternately. There is a very good reason for this. Too many motorcyclists form a very bad habit of being competent in left turns and incompetent on making right turns. Since we are interested in forming good habits, this is the place to form your first. After the 10 to the left and to the right, do 10 more each to the left and right with turns, but this time shifting from first to second gear somewhere on the straightaway or the turn. At the end of this time you should have done approximately 60 drills and you should now be ready for further adventures. If it is at all possible, I suggest constant repetition of these until they become second nature. These previous 60 drills are the fundamental and basic maneuvers of learning to drive a motorcycle. The *Intermediate Drill* is next.

The *Intermediate Drill* includes such things as serpentine driving. This is best accomplished by placing standing bricks 15 feet apart, at least 6 of them, and the motorcyclist weaves in and out of the bricks slowly in first gear. This will develop his balance control and it will also develop his ability to control his clutch, his throttle, and his brakes while going through the serpentine area. If he has a very large machine such as the 750cc, I suggest stretching the bricks out a little bit so that the S turns are shallower. This should be practiced back and forth at least 10 times. If the cyclist becomes proficient, he should try shifting or increasing the speed.

The second part of the *Intermediate Drill* is the *Tunnel.* Place about 20 or 30 bricks opposite each other and 3 feet apart. There should be about 8 feet between bricks in each row, making a tunnel 3 feet wide and 80 or more feet long. If the bike is small, narrow the tunnel down to about 2 feet. If it is possible, lay a straight line down the middle with masking tape. The object is that the cyclist is to enter the tunnel and go down at a slow speed without wandering off and touching the bricks. Even if he does touch the bricks they will fall over and no harm will be done. The purpose of drills one and two in the *Intermediate Stage* is to duplicate the conditions that he will find when he takes a driver's test. These are two of the driver's test requirements in most states that have motorcycle driving tests.

Drill Three Intermediate. Practice driving down the *tunnel* and coming to a dead stop without lockup or skid. This develops skill in coming to an upright stop with the motorcycle under control. It requires that the rear brake be applied just a fraction of a second before the front brake and that the braking be very very smooth. If the braking is too stiff on the rear brake lever, the motorcycle will skid. Applying the front

Instructor is pointing out directional signals and stoplight assembly on training bike. Student should be able to make turns with the directional signals as well as hand signals.

<

Serpentine practice under the supervision of an instructor. Bricks are laid
out about 15 feet apart. Student travels through in first gear, turning 360°
at each end and going back in the opposite direction. Serpentine practice
is continued by shifting into second gear or putting the bricks closer together. This causes much more maneuvering by the student driver.

brake on dry flat surfaces too soon won't cause any obvious
problems, but it is not a good idea since if you did the same
thing on wet pavement, sand, or snow, you would probably
cause a "lockup" condition that might cause a spill. So, practice
with both brakes, leading a little bit with the rear brake, and
increase your speed until you have developed good control.
This is also part of the driver's test. Never brake on a curve.

Drill Four Intermediate. This requires making a figure
"8." You should do at least 10 of these 35-foot circles. The average highway is about 40 feet wide. This isn't an exercise to
make you proficient at U turns, but an exercise to develop your
skill in controlling your driving in tight circles. This should be
practiced for at least 10 figure 8s and this is the end of the
Intermediate Stage of learning to drive a motorcycle.

To sum up this chapter, the *Primary* and *Intermediate*
Drills are listed in consecutive order and in the order in which
they should be learned. Before anybody goes out into traffic
conditions, these drills should be committed to memory. There
are a few other points that should be practiced during this
particular stage.

One of these is the business of giving *hand signals* for
turns and stopping. A car will remain upright. A motorcycle
will not. As soon as one hand is taken off the left handlebar
to do the signaling, it poses another problem in balance for
the rider. There are 3 universal signs. The left hand is held
up in the air 90° to the elbow—this signifies a right turn. If
you wish to point the finger slightly, this is also acceptable.
I have noticed many cyclists make a slight "arc," pointing
slightly over their heads. This seems to be acceptable too.
Perhaps it is even more descriptive.

<

Serpentine driving at slow speed. She will make wide circles as shown here.
In serpentine driving at high speeds, there is hardly a movement from the
straight and narrow to maneuver these bricks.

A *left turn* is the arm straight out with the elbow locked or close to it. Here too, there are minor variations such as a pointed index finger, and I have also seen cyclists use a piston-type motion with the hand. A slight bend at the elbow extending it straight out going back and forth.

The universal *stop sign* is the hand down. This is usually extended at a 45° angle from the shoulder with a straight arm and the palm facing back indicating a stop.

The last hand signal used refers to traffic behind you. It is the *pass me* signal. This is a rolling motion of the left arm in a forward direction. This is sometimes used after a *stop* signal.

There are other signals that motorcyclists give themselves, but they are signs of recognition such as the clenched fist with the left hand. This is a universal signal well recognized and it is a mark of recognition between fellow sportsmen. Just don't shake it. You may have more of a problem than you can handle.

For the last 5 or 6 years, motorcyclists have carried on a small public relations campaign with young children. I think it is important enough to put into this book because I believe in it, too. It is the V signal to small children when you come to a stoplight or when you see them along the sides of the road or in the back of a station wagon. Apparently, the children very quickly understand this form of recognition from an adult to a child. And many times I have found that the child initiates the signal before I have a chance to. By this simple recognition, we are planting a subliminal thought in the minds of children that motorcycling is something they might want to do when they are older.

Practicing these hand signals while driving should be done in the parking lot and be included in the *Intermediate Stage* of learning to ride. Even though all manufacturers or importers are required to include directional signals, quite sophisticated ones too, it is still important for you to be thoroughly aware of how to make proper hand signals.

Practice leaning, for all turns are made not by the turning of the handlebars, but by leaning with the bike. A slight imperceptible lean or "body English" can do marvelous things with the maneuvering of a motorcycle. This will be explored more fully in the chapter on "Defensive Driving."

A right-turn signal is given by making a slight arc from the shoulder over to the top of the head or pointing straight up. This is in addition to a right-hand signal light.

A left-hand turn pointing to left, arm straight out. Once again, an addition to a left-turn signal.

Webco gloves are faced on one side with white and the other black. In this case, this particular signal shows a full-stop position. Note also that although the driver is waiting presumably at a light or to make a turn, the passenger keeps her feet up.

Motorcyclists exchange a greeting. Usually the closed fist or the victory sign, always with the left hand.

5

Riding Defensively

D RIVING defensively is something that all drivers, automobile, motorcycle, or whatever, should do, but it is much more important for the motorcyclist to drive defensively because of his greater exposure to accidents. The chance of a driver's being injured in an accident involving a motorcycle is greater than any other type of motor vehicle accident. Eight out of ten persons suffer some type of injury when they have been involved in an accident riding a motorcycle. It should be quite obvious due to the configuration of the motorcycle. A simple tap on the rear of a motorcycle by a car will cause no damage to the car, but could very easily cause the motorcyclist to lose balance and crash. Interestingly, 45 percent of injuries sustained involve damage to the head.

There are six vulnerable positions or "directions of possible accident": a car coming toward the motorcyclist in the opposite lane; a car coming from the motorcyclist's left broadside, usually at an intersection; a car coming from the motorcyclist's right, usually from an intersection or driveway; and a car coming from the rear, either tailgating or passing you, the motorcyclist. The other two would be left oblique and right oblique, or coming at a 45° angle to the motorcycle.

The motorcyclist should be aware of these six situations and have already figured out defensive or evasive maneuvers designed to prevent the accident.

These I will call "Collision Avoidance Maneuvers." Automobile drivers and motorcyclists have long assumed that the motorcycle can outmaneuver a car. It has been proven that this is not so, that the car may, in fact, have greater maneuverability than the motorcycle. It is simply that the motorcycle has "apparent" maneuverability due to its small size and shape. In studies by various motorcycle safety groups, however, it appears that motorcyclists generally suffer from two fears. One of them is the fear of front-wheel lockup when the front brake is applied. This fear is justified when the machine is old or perhaps has an old drum-type front wheel. With today's modern front-wheel disc brake, a lockup is rarer, but these remarks are relative to the care and attention that the driver gives his braking.

The other consideration isn't exactly a fear, it's overconfidence. Overconfidence or a misunderstanding of the motorcycle's ability for evasive action.

These two emotional considerations work to the motorcyclist's detriment in accident-avoidance maneuvering.

There is a third problem caused by little or no or improper training in exactly what happens when a motorcycle makes a turn. When analyzing how a turn is made with either a motorcycle or a bicycle, one becomes aware of the fact that the front wheel must be "out-tracked" or "displaced" from the normal tracking procedure of the rear wheel following the front. In a turn, say to the right, as in collision avoidance maneuvers, the front wheel is first turned to the *left* almost imperceptibly, then the motorcyclist turns to the right and leans into the turn. This quick left momentary maneuver displaces the front wheel and as the cyclist turns to the right and leans into the turn, the front stays "out-tracked" for duration of the turn. At the end of the turn, the front wheel must be "in-tracked" for recover-

My gal Sal doesn't look too happy about having to pose in what looks like a motorcycle accident. (She's driving the car.) Can't really blame her. This picture illustrates two important points; if you have any opportunity at all to avoid an accident, it's best to lay the machine down, that is, slide-kelly-slide. Motorcycles with crash or safety bars on them will protect your lower leg. This is another reason why padded leather shoulder, elbows, and hips are sewn into good leather outfits. Notice the contact points here. Had this been a real accident, he would have hit his left shoulder and head. Another good reason for wearing good boots.

ing and, here too, the front wheel is turned opposite to the recovery point.

It sounds weird, but this "cornering" or "turning" is accomplished with the front wheel displaced in regard to the tracking of the rear wheel. Without an understanding of this action, a cyclist won't have as fast a reaction time as needed in collision-avoidance turns as well as in general motorcycle driving.

This photograph of the vehicle cocked to the right is to illustrate the fact that in a turn to the right, or left for that matter, the front wheel and the rear wheel do not track in the same parallel paths. (See text for explanation.)

By now it is well known to all motorcyclists and many lay people that there is a psychological problem with the automobile driver in that he has a great deal of difficulty "seeing" a motorcycle. I for one claim that this is a subliminal problem in that the motorcycle does not make an impression on the car driver's consciousness. This is because the driver of the car is looking for a large 18 or 20 foot rectangular box, 5 or 6 feet high and 6 or 7 feet wide. The smaller machine and cycle rider does not register on his subconscious as a vehicle to be considered. Consequently he pulls out into a lane of traffic from a driveway or side road and crosses in front of you or pulls around you or any number of things that appear to ignore you. He is not driving arrogantly. It really has nothing personal to do with you as a motorcycle driver. It just isn't registering in his head.

Pulling out of intersections or driveways is a big cause of accidents. Your lights should be on, as the headlight is in this photograph taken during daylight hours. Be ever aware of the pullout from your right; drivers often don't see you.

Same view at night. A large adequate air horn or Hella-Type horn is best. This coupled with a powerful light might warn the driver, but be ever aware that he or she might not hear and see you.

There is another problem that psychologists have become aware of recently in regard to motorcycle accidents and this is the problem of hostility. Some automotive drivers are hostile toward motorcyclists. For some reason they resent their intrusion into the cars' driving lanes, and a motorcyclist driving defensively should be aware that this phenomenon could exist in a driver and be prepared for abnormal movements on the part of the motorists in his proximity. Remember that a motorcyclist has one third the visual area of an automobile. That means he is 66 percent less visible than a car.

These points outlined above place an added responsibility on the motorcyclist to learn to drive defensively. This has been hammered home in all sorts of safety pamphlets, instruction books, state traffic law books, and other material. Although I don't want to be redundant, I would like to condense a good deal of the information in other pamphlets and crystallize just what a motorcyclist can do to be considered a good defensive driver.

Just as we understand that there is a psychological problem with the automobile driver in regard to the motorcyclists, there are psychological problems with the motorcyclist. One is a sense of power, and it is a mistaken sense of power. A sense of complete command and self-assurance is attributed to the fact that there are no blind spots to inhibit your field of vision. Steering is extremely easy, controls are simple, and response instantaneous in acceleration and braking. It has been mentioned before that a motorcyclist can out-accelerate and out-brake any car around. A cyclist who develops perfect skill and manipulation of these controls can really move that bike. If he uses these skills cautiously and to his own advantage, he can preserve his own skin.

When I say that the motorcycle can accelerate and out-brake any car around I'm talking about the mechanical potential capability of the motorcycle. However, if the cyclist for one reason or another has poor reaction time, or, for example, simply will not use his front brake because he has been programmed through reading many articles on motorcycling to believe that the use of the front brake could be or can be dangerous, then he simply won't use the capability of the motorcycle in braking. If a motorcyclist has a modern motorcycle with a disc brake and he is a skilled cyclist, other conditions being equal, he could stop that motorcycle in less time and space than most automobiles.

Let's talk for a moment on "Collision-Avoidance Maneuvers." To the average neophyte cyclist, a turn seems relatively simple. Just turn the handlebars in the direction you want to go and lean with it. But there is a vast difference between the turn performed by a novice cyclist and real pro who understands his cycle. Pitted against each other, you would find that the pro would be able to make his turn more quickly and steeply in trying to avoid a car coming out of a side street, crossing an intersection, or coming out of a driveway. This could mean the difference between an accident and the avoidance of one.

To understand exactly how much of a "lean" one can make at varying speeds, one must analyze the "tracking of the front and rear wheels." As an example, two-wheeled vehicles don't track the same in a turn. By that I mean that the wheels don't follow each other one after the other in a turn. During a left turn the front would be out from the track made by the rear wheel. If you analzye the beginning of a turn, you will notice that just before the cyclist turns and leans to the left, there is an almost imperceptible movement of the front fork to the right. The purpose of this is to offset the front wheel, or "out-track" the front wheel, by the steering mechanism opposite the direction of the turn. Then the left turn of the handlebar plus the lean can be greater and therefore quicker and take less distance than had the motorcycle not been "out-tracked." Conversely, when you come out of the turn you must in-track to bring yourself upright, and obviously the same applies in the opposite direction.

Many skilled cyclists are not aware of this. Those who had the privilege of reading or watching others, especially flat trackers and road racers will find that they're very well aware of this effect and use it to good advantage on the track.

One of the ways in which a man can learn to be a good defensive driver is first to learn to drive a car. I hope that everybody who learns to drive a motorcycle has already driven an automobile. This will indicate the individual's competency to react properly to traffic situations.

Youngsters who learn to ride motorcycles without having driven automobiles don't have previous experience in traffic, and this is definitely a disadvantage. Driver education courses teach new automobile drivers laws and rules of the road and traffic situations, but a motorcyclist usually picks up his information from an older rider. Whenever I hear of someone learning to drive a motorcycle on the road before he learns to drive a car, I am wary.

I would classify defensive riding and driving as being "suspicious" of every other driver on the road and being prepared to take evasive action at any time and I would assume that the automobile driver does not see me. Knowing what we know about automobile drivers, at least we have a distinct advantage. If we assume that we are unseen, then we should make ourselves visible.

One of the ways that I think is important is the attachment of a good pair of horns. The little motorcycle "beep beep" is a ridiculous excuse for a warning device. It may be required to save your life or prevent serious injury in an accident someday. The horn should be of the type that is reminiscent of a large car or a small truck. I am not suggesting air horns with all sorts of paraphernalia, although they do make these as accessories for motorcycles. I am thinking in terms of something like the Hella Twin Horns, which have a safety factor in another area—animals chasing motorcycles. These horns are used much more liberally than you would use them if you were driving a car. Driving defensively means that you must assume that you are not seen; therefore, you must warn somebody crossing in front of you or passing. If you wish to pass, the driver may not see you and you could have been in his blind spot. A blast on these horns will alert him at least to look for you. The first thing he is looking for is the large vehicle, but at least it wakes him up from his reverie.

Another feature, not popular with a lot of motorcyclists but required by New York State and four others, is to leave your headlight on. There are very good reasons for the law, such as to draw attention to you and your motorcycle. I heartily agree with the law, although I feel that I would reply more on overall defensive driving. The horns and light I would consider additional safety factors.

Speaking about leaving your headlights on during the daytime, remember to keep your rpms up. Most alternators cut in about 2100 rpm, so keep your rpm up when you come to a stoplight or stop sign. Otherwise, you may be discharging your battery. Most motorcycle batteries, generators, and alternators were not meant for such heavy use. Buy a bigger battery as needed.

It's a well-known fact that most motorcycle electric and lighting systems are inadequate from a safety point of view. I'm not too sure whether this subject of headlights belongs under the chapter on safety or defensive driving. They're almost synonymous, but there are very few motorcycles that have adequate lighting. Headlights, of course, and taillights are the primary considerations. The taillights are getting bigger and they do look monstrous on the back of some cycles. But believe me, as big as they are they're still too small because they're not surrounded with something else that's visible. The headlights leave a lot to be desired. Some progress is being made in dual headlight mechanisms, such as two-bulb, quartz-halogen lamps, for example, and the new high-output low-energy bulbs being invented every day. Harley-Davidson is considered as the motorcycle with the best battery, generator, alternator, electric system, and the best headlights. Yamaha has produced a marvelous feature in their new large bikes: should the high beam or low beam go out, the other will automatically switch on, an excellent safety feature. Statistics show that motorcycles are 40 percent more visible when they leave

Side view of full-dressed Harley in beautiful condition. Big electrics, car-size battery, best lighting of any bike made. When the saddlebags and pannier are loaded, no problem with wobble. Beautiful design.

their lights on during the daylight hours. At the time of the writing of this book, five states have what we call "headlight laws." My information on material put out by the Motorcycle Industry Counsel indicates that almost all states have proposed legislation in this area. It is only fair for me to assume that it will be a year or two before everybody will be required to leave headlights on during daylight hours. This means the motorcycle industry will have to improve their electrical systems which in turn means more cost to be passed on to the consumer.

At night the visibility of a motorcycle is almost non-existent. Anyone who drives with one headlight and an ordinary taillight and a black leather jacket has got to be flirting with the devil. An oncoming motorist cannot judge either distance or speed by one headlight. That same oncoming motorist might consider you a car with one light out, but which one?

I've recently read of a test engineer from Chrysler Corporation who had a high-reflectance jump suit made out of silver Scotchlite. He was driving a BMW, and I am positive he intended to be seen.

Defensive driving requires anticipating a problem before it takes place. Anticipate that children in residential areas often dash into the roads from between parked cars. They, too, when looking to run across the road, are not thinking in terms of motorcycles and could very easily run out in front of you. They are looking for cars and trucks. Their subconscious is not tuned to a motorcyclist. Anticipate that they will run out in front of you, and drive accordingly.

A quiet machine, meaning good mufflers, is another feature of defensive driving. Since loud mufflers distract motorists and startle them, they sometimes cause them to swerve unintentionally.

Drive so that you are visible when you are behind a car. Don't park in the driver's blind spot. In general you should be driving to the left of the center of your lane for three good reasons. One, so you could be seen by the driver ahead of you, two, so you can see oncoming traffic, and three, so oncoming traffic can see you.

If you do not have direction signals, use your hand signals. Also, use them in conjunction with your directional and stop-light signals. This will draw attention to you. One thing that I do at night is change to a two-sided glove. One side is black and one side is a light tan. These are motorcycle Moto-Cross gloves with a rib of rubber following the line of each finger protecting the knuckles and the back of the hand. These are excellent at night because I turn my palm back to the driver behind me and he can see the white gloved hand in his headlights. For the same reason I use only a white or silver crash helmet. It may be very fashionable to have a black bike with a black helmet, but you may very well be overrun by a speeding motorist (see section on Night Driving).

Don't drive beyond the limit of your headlight. There are often all sorts of debris on the street such as dead animals, old mufflers, pieces of truck tires, and blocks of wood; these are the most common. Hitting one of these at 50 or 60 or more mph can mean a bad spill. If you recover from your own spill, you could be run over by the cars behind you.

Whatever you do, don't ever take a motorcycle out on a freeway, turnpike, or limited access highway unless you have

These are Webco gloves, white on one side, black on the other, with heavy rubber protectors over the fingers. These are usually made for Moto-Crossers.

a minimum of 350cc and are not overloaded with luggage so that you are unable to pass a car successfully up to 80 mph (see information on Consumer Information Part 375 included in your instruction book).

Never ride between two lanes of cars. Not only is it against the law, but motorcycles have been known to be hit by long rearview mirrors and by trucks or cars that carry trailers or campers. It is also discourteous to other drivers. When passing, always give liberal signals. Give yourself more space than you think you need and enter the new traffic lane at a speed equal to or exceeding that of the passing traffic and don't cut in too sharply on the car you just passed. The rule is, wait until you can see him in your rearview mirror before you pull in.

State laws vary regarding passing. Passing on the right is illegal in a number of states. Whether or not it is a law

Illegal. Motorcycle is out of lane squeezing in between curbing and line of traffic. You are required to maintain your position in a line of traffic. Making your own special lane either between two lanes of cars or alongside a lane is illegal, besides being extremely dangerous.

it is a good practice never to pass on the right. Stay two seconds away from the vehicle you are passing and pass on the left. Never pass on a curve or a hill where you can't see oncoming traffic.

When you are doing any road riding, you have the control as to keeping a special distance behind the car ahead of you. About 40 feet per 10 mph of speed is the rule of the thumb. It is twice what it is for a car, even though you have better braking, visibility, and better acceleration. If you tailgate a car ahead of you and the guy behind you is tailgating you, you are in a box. Just be careful it isn't made of pine. So, keep that distance from the car ahead of you.

Tailgating other vehicles is not a good idea for many reasons. The driver of a car may see an object in the road and straddle it. If you don't have distance between the car and yourself, that object goes right under your front wheel. If it is large enough it could throw you. If that guy ahead of you puts his brakes on fast because of somebody or something darting out into the road, you are going to climb up on top of his roof, so keep your distance.

Passing on curves is obviously dangerous. You haven't got the visibility. Don't get impressed with your super XTL 750cc something or other. Sure it will move and sure it will accelerate, but as long as you don't know what is coming around that curve no matter how much power you have, you can't depend on the speed alone; it just isn't a good safety habit.

Passing at an intersection is an invitation to disaster. There could be three cars coming from three different directions and all three of them could be "blind" to you. You have tripled your chance of getting killed.

Defensive driving requires that you know what is ahead of you before you pass anyway. In a car you could be partially surprised when coming upon steel grates or railroad tracks around a bend. You can't afford to take that chance on a motorcycle. It requires a special technique. You have to cross tracks at 90° or you may be "rutted." If you cross this sort of thing partially parallel, you might skid or catch your wheel in one of the tracks. The best thing to do when you get on a grating is to reduce speed and neither accelerate or brake. You don't want to break that traction!

Check your mirrors constantly in this passing situation. Especially when you are overtaking an automobile or other vehicle. Make sure the driver's aware of your presence. Make sure he either sees you in his rearview mirror or sideview mirror, and make sure by using your horn and/or lights or everything.

When you are turning a corner, do all of your braking before you reach the corner. Once you start leaning and are making that turn you need no braking. This is especially true if the surface is slippery or covered by loose gravel or dirt. You may cause the bike to lose traction. If it is necessary to reduce your speed, apply your rear brakes very gently. Leaning with your body, of course, helps in turning the bike.

Driving on high bridges during a heavy wind or on highways when it is windy can cause "buffeting." You just about lean into the wind when all of a sudden the wind stops for a second and you go right out of your lane. The best way to drive in a high wind is very cautiously, keeping your profile low and using as low a speed as you can drive at and still stay with the flow of traffic.

There is another type of buffeting, and this is getting behind a big truck where you get into "vortices." These are spinning turbulences of air behind the truck. Directly behind the truck is a vacuum. If the truck is one of those large Fruehauf trailer trucks, that vacuum will be about 30 feet. It is shaped at one end like the back of the truck, then narrows down to a triangular cone point about 30 feet back. It is hollow and somewhat of a vacuum. Some drivers of cars and motorcyclists get into this vacuum area for warmth or to get out of the wind and spray of everything else, but at the speeds they are going in order to give you 30 feet, you are tailgating —a very dangerous practice.

On road driving and highway driving, leaves blowing around don't represent much of a problem. Wet leaves on the ground do. They affect your traction. (That will come in another chapter.) Pieces of garbage and newspaper flying around could blind you.

To sum up some of the features of defensive driving, you could say that motorcyclists must have a high degree of concentration. Riding a motorcycle on a freeway is not the place to dope off. It should be a matter of pride to develop your defensive driving skill so that you are the master of all situations except the completely unknown. Remember, drive as if nobody can see you.

6

Road Safety

ROAD safety is more important for the road motorcyclist than it is for the automobile driver. Four wheels give an automobile some immunity from special hazards and some insulation in accidents as attested to by the fact that 8 out of 10 motorcycle accidents produce injuries to the driver of the motorcycle. Road safety is essentially "the way in which you drive," not the mechanical manipulation of controls, and it is very closely related to the previous chapter on defensive riding. A good start toward driving safely would be to know the motor vehicle rules and regulations in your state as well as those of adjacent states. As an example, some states do not allow passing on the right on roads having only one or two lanes in any one direction, but if there are three lanes in one direction, you may pass either to the left or to the right. If you went into an adjacent state where this rule was not a regulation, you should still drive as if it were. Many drivers are startled by someone coming up on the right side, especially if they are from those states that have a "no passing on the right" law.

Creating a "third lane" by riding down the middle or along the shoulder of a road is illegal in all 50 states. It is also extremely dangerous. The car in the right lane just might decide to turn right and there is a period when you are coming up on him that you are in his blind spot.

As mentioned before, you obviously don't pass on a curve or on a hill unless you can see oncoming traffic and have a clear road. In excess of the distance needed to pass and per Regulation 375, if you know, for example, that you can make a low-speed pass in 370 feet, you should have at least double that distance as a cushion against an oncoming car. On a high-speed pass, where you might need 850 feet, you are going to need 1700 or more feet or a third of a mile. That is a lot of distance. If you know your regulation as it pertains to your bike, that is, what distance it takes and how much time for you to make a low-speed and a high-speed pass, you can estimate these distances and thereby know the limitations of your bike.

This photograph is one of a series of a driver preparing to pass a camper. The rider first looks in his rearview mirror and, as soon as the truck passes, throws on his left directional signal.

Driver preparing to pass the camper. The truck having passed him, he is now starting to move out into passing lane.

Using his directional signals, as well as his hand, he is moving into left or passing lane.

He's now in the passing lane except that he has to "occupy" it. That means he has to be to the left of the center of the lane.

He has started to move up on the camper. However, the car directly behind him is tailgating him. This is one of the most dangerous positions. (See chapter 5, Sixth Position of an Accident.)

He has moved over in front of the camper, has gotten rid of the tailgater, and he's riding in the proper position in his lane.

All riding should be done left of the center in his lane for several reasons. One is, it gives him and oncoming traffic visibility; he is seen and can see. Number two, the vehicle ahead can pick him up in the rearview and side mirrors. Number three, he's staying out of the darkest area, which is the center. It is usually loaded with fumes and grease which could be slippery.

As pointed out in other chapters, your brakes are superior to those of cars and your front brake is really superior, but remember, when you pull that front brake hard, you can't steer. Good braking requires the use of both brakes and you are going to use them in traffic. Using brakes "wisely" means using them judiciously as well. You don't just pull the power on a slick surface or oil spots or sand. You brake before you lean into a curve—not while you are in it.

You must anticipate road surfaces. As you gain experience with either a motorcycle or a car, but mostly on a motorcycle, you will discover that you become very adept at reading the topography. You will know a country road can turn into areas where there is sand along the sides. If it is in the Northwest, it is also going to have ice patches until spring. You know you could round a corner and run into sand that had been spread by sanding trucks. You should be able to know what to expect if you have traveled a road for any length at all. So, you drive anticipating these particular problems. Because they do not show in any one day doesn't mean you don't continuously look for them.

Driving safely requires you to get into the left of your middle lane, using either your turn signal or your hand signals or both, and coming to a slow stop. A good trick to draw attention is to lightly tap your foot brake with your right foot, this will cause a flashing of your brake light and alert the drivers behind you.

I don't think this problem will come up too often for a motorcyclist, but one of the big problems on the new freeways is the "moper." He is a slowpoke. He enters traffic from an entrance ramp going too slow and below the speed of normal traffic flow, thus forcing fast-moving vehicles to slow down. This causes an accordionlike effect that has been known to cause many accidents. When you pull out of a "Yield" sign, pull smartly into traffic, attempting to be at the normal speed of traffic by the time you are in the right-hand lane after having left the entrance ramp.

The moper also shows up as a pain in the neck when he is in a line of traffic. Obviously he can't exist in the inside lane or passing lane, and he does sometimes clog up the slow traffic lane. Some states have laws prohibiting people from going less than 40 mph. These "Mopery Laws" or "Slow Driver Laws" are designed to keep the traffic moving at a constant

flow. Some motorcycles are so overloaded that they just can't pass that easily. Still, almost any bike with a passenger should be able to go 40 mph and stay safely in the right-hand lane at say, 50 mph. So long as the motorcyclist doesn't attempt to do any passing he should be quite safe in that lane.

Group riding is always dangerous. Even 6, 8, or 10 motorcycles scattered zigzag fashion in one lane can hold up a whole line of cars because in order to pass the group of motorcycles, a car needs two or three times its normal passing distance. Sometimes, that much highway just isn't available. It is often best to break up strings into smaller groups. Avoid getting lost by having certain rendezvous points or having the leader wait at a certain intersection until all bikes have finally caught up.

In some states there is a law against stringing out and blocking traffic, even though you are riding safely and legally and singly, if there is a group of motorcycles that string out without sufficient distance between them for a car to pass one and duck in. So, by keeping the distance short by another motorcyclist you effectively block passing drivers and thereby break the law. Nobody, but nobody, should ever pass in a group. Two-at-a-time passing a vehicle is a no-no!

Just recently the United States has started to change all of its signs to a more visual description of the conditions that exist, using fewer spelled-out words. This accords with world organizations and Europe in particular, which have had descriptive symbols for years. As an example, the stop sign is 8-sided. The diamond and yellow type sign is used for warning signs with descriptions.

The triangle is used exclusively for yield signs, and the rectangle is used for information signs. The circular yellow sign with the black cross and the two Rs will remain as the railroad symbol. The information signs, square or rectangular, will also be descriptive. They also call these prohibitive signs, such as: No Right Turn, No Left Turn, and No U Turn.

<

Most of the year, the edges of many secondary roads contain sand as shown in this photograph. This is another good reason for driving in the left of center of your lane. In northern parts of the country this sand is left over from the sanding of roads after snowstorms.

International pavement markings are now changing. The color white is going to be used for separating traffic lanes moving in the same direction and yellow lines are going to be used for separating traffic lanes moving in opposite directions. It will take awhile for these to be painted all over the country, but learn about them now and expect them.

In two previous chapters there has been something said about proper lighting for night driving. My caution here is, in any night driving you must be alert to the fact that there may be something on the road that cannot be seen or picked up by a headlight. A car can pass over it and it isn't disastrous, but motorcycles that hit an object usually take an instant spill.

Nobody likes a show-off. Dancing in and out of traffic, weaving, inattention to your driving, carrying on conversations with your passenger, riding no hands, all of these things are the mark of the immature motorcyclist. The true sportsman is a professional. You can almost tell by the way he sits in his saddle and the way he handles his machine that he has the mark of the perfectionist about him. If you wish to be admired for your motorcycle driving skill, it is the smooth unobtrusive professionalism that shows up in traffic that impresses everybody.

An experienced automobile driver can watch a motorcycle traveling at about the same speed for just a few minutes in traffic and instantly tell. He can tell by the way you move in and out of lanes. He can tell by the way you keep your distance. He can tell whether your application of the throttle is jerky or your braking is crash-type braking or whether you are a smooth perfectionist. There are many ways in which you can "show off" your skill as a motorcyclist, but your attention to safety on the road is appreciated by other users. Drive wisely and therefore safely.

If you don't drive safely you will be legislated into driving safely. The accident statistics on motorcycles in the United States have been labeled "epidemic." Even by the time this book is in print, there will be law after law enacted. Most of these laws are well intentioned. Many are needed. Some are foolish.

The future of motorcycling safety includes a whole new set of features. Let me here and now list some of these new designs of the future:

Shows the new and old road signs and directions. These are appropriate for the motorcyclist as well as the automobilist.

OLD

NEW

NEW ROAD SIGNS
COMING YOUR WAY

OLD

NEW

OLD	NEW

DO NOT ENTER

| NO RIGHT TURN | |

NO LEFT TURN

NO U TURN

KNOW YOUR ROAD SIGNS

THE BASIC SHAPES AND WHAT THEY MEAN

OCTAGON
USED EXCLUSIVELY FOR
STOP SIGNS

TRIANGLE
USED EXCLUSIVELY FOR
YIELD SIGNS

DIAMOND
USED FOR WARNING
SIGNS

RECTANGLE
USED FOR INFORMATION
SIGNS

NEW ROAD SIGNS COMING YOUR WAY

THE MOST IMPORTANT
TRAFFIC SIGN,
THE STOP SIGN
WILL REMAIN RED

OLD

NEW

New Gas Tank:

Will have a rubber inner bag and the recessed screw-in or bayonet-type cap. Accident tests have shown that where a motorcycle has been involved in a head-on collision or has rammed the rear of a stopped vehicle, the present gasoline tanks rupture, the snap-down cap flies open and as the cyclist rides low over the bike in the collision, he suffers pelvic damage from the protruding gas cap. He's completely enveloped in gasoline and gasoline vapor. As he and the gas leave the bike, he is injured as he crosses all of the paraphernalia on the front end—steering damper, handlebar, triple fork, and crown.

Plastic Fenders:

The jagged edges of ripped metal fenders have torn much flesh. It is hoped that plastic fenders will give in an accident and prevent some of this carnage.

New foot pegs will not fold and crush the instep but would protect the foot. Foot pegs should be able to skid at least 25 feet on concrete without bending or breaking.

New Type of Tires:

Tires painted with reflective material imbedded into the rubber on the sidewalls so that visibility is heightened at night. Tires that are tubeless and are locked on the rims with either tire locks or bead dimples. Disc brakes with complete antilock devices.

New Horns:

With a minimum of 105 decibels at 25 feet.

Helmets:

Will eventually be designed so that they pass one overall United States regulation. Helmets will be covered with reflective material such as Scotchlite.

Motorcycle Suits:

Special jump suits will be required to be worn at night, and be made of a special high-reflectance material such as Scotchlite.

Unicolor Motorcycle:

It's entirely possible that someday everyone will be required to drive a cycle with perhaps a single color such as "International Orange."

Some of these things are abhorrent to motorcyclists, especially those who consider themselves "purists."

7

Personal Safety

IT has been known for many years by motorcyclists that wearing a good set of leathers is like having a "second skin" and that leathers are a "must" for the Moto-Crosser or the racing driver. On the highway, the leathers are good for a short trip and in some cases on long trips if you have accessory rain gear to fit over them. There is nothing heavier than wet leather, and leather is not a protection against either snow or rain. One-piece leather suits are excellent in that they prevent wind from driving up and billowing the jacket part in a two-piece outfit. Tailored leathers going tight to the ankles with zippers and tight to the wrists are attractive and professional looking. Worn with gauntlet gloves and proper boots a very commanding "hero figure" emerges. Leathers are good windbreakers as everybody knows.

Longer trips require a different type of wearing apparel. One I like the best, summer or winter, is a Sears Arctic One-Piece Suit worn over your regular clothes or even your leathers. This zips down to the ankle and to the wrists and the zippers go both ways up and down. It is exceedingly warm. I drive my personal machine in 18° weather. This is my cutoff point for driving. Below this, I feel a little bit too chilled. This still makes me a winter driver and it is possible because of these "snowsuits."

As often happens, one sport steals from another. We use skiers' gloves, face masks, and goggles, and often some of their suits for cold riding. The snowmobile has contributed the snowsuit to us and often special types of cold weather boots.

Summertime protection for a rider. Proper boots, good heavy corduroy or whipcord trousers, reinforced leather jacket with zippered gussets, flip-top face shield and a full coverage helmet, good serviceable, finger-protecting gloves.

Boots bring up a problem of footgear. Leather serves as a good protection in the event of a spill but the prime purpose of your boot is going to be protection against weather. Especially the cold. Some companies sell fleece-lined boots. When properly oiled with neat's-foot oil liberally worked into the leather and then polished off with Langlitz Leathers dressing, you have the combination of good looks, all-weather protection, and extreme warmth. The boots are zipped up the rear. Laced boots such as engineers' boots with hooks and eyes for laces, are all right for woods drivers, but they are rather impractical on the road. There are many regular boots that can be purchased in

This picture shows what the well-dressed winter driver wears: a full-length snowmobile suit, tucked into fleece-lined leather zip-up boots, with ski mask worn under helmet.

any footwear store. The problem with these is that your feet get cold due to inaction. Even in the summer on very long trips, it is best to wear good warm footwear.

I carry my snowsuit on the back of my bike all summer long and on a trip. These snowsuits are waterproof, and zipping into one of these "snugglies" places you in a cocoon of extreme warmth and comfort and completely protects you from head to toe from the elements.

Winter "waffle" underwear is good all year around, not only as a protection in the event of spills but to prevent the inevitable draft. One of the big problems with the motorcyclist is an intestinal flu caused from sitting on cold saddles. Not many cyclists identify their problem with this cause, but it is a prevalent one. Gloves should always be gauntlet type, winter and summer, although they can be lighter weight in the summer. The gauntlet prevents the wind from going up a sleeve. Here again, we have crossed over to the skier and the snowmobile for some of their equipment.

The helmet should definitely have the *flip-up type plastic face shield*. Nowadays, these are bonded with Hexadron, an antifogging chemical which prevents a mist from forming on the inside either by your breath in cold weather or by fog in the summer.

The flip-top shield is vital as opposed to those that are snapped on permanently.

Many riders have been killed by their face shields' fogging up at night in the spring and fall when valleys have fog or dew. You drive over one hill into the valley and your face shield fogs over instantly. It only takes a few seconds and you are unable to see. If you can't rip that face shield off fast, you just bought the cake. If you survive one of these, and I did, from then on you will only buy the flip-up-type face shield. If you wear glasses, as I do, you have a double problem. You could also be fogging your glasses. Believe me, I have ripped those off in a hurry, too. The best protection against fogging is one of the new silicone additives that can either be sprayed or rubbed onto glasses and face mask. They effectively prevent fogging. However, they do condense the moisture into a fluid that runs down your face. A little discomfort is far better than an impending disaster.

In a recent analysis of helmets, out of 100 different brands on the market only 11 were approved. A "Z" certificate is no longer good enough. If you can get a "Snell Foundation" rat-

Low-lying fog in spring and fall will fog up or mist up your face shield. If it's permanently attached, you are blind. This is another reason why windshields should be cut lower than the driver's eyes. The shield should be on a swivel able to be snapped down and unsnapped quickly.

ing, you will find you have a better helmet. So often people buy helmets for looks and a helmet doesn't do much good unless it is buckled. In the woods a helmet has a "beak" or "duckbill." These are for the purpose of brushing aside willows, sticks, and branches by tipping the rider's head down. The beak is not often worn by the road rider because of the need of the face shield. A face shield also acts as a warmer, especially in the winter, but I do not recommend the bulbous type that encases you in some sort of "man from Mars cocoon." There are adequate face shields that are curved in one direction and have an antifogging device and the ability to be flipped up. You will have to experiment with two or three different types until you find the one you like.

I do not recommend different color face shields. They give you a false feeling of security. If they are yellow or blue, you are unable to judge weather; the very dark green or smoky ones that protect your eyes from the glare of the sun are simply too dark and can dilate your pupils abnormally, causing eye fatigue and eyestrain.

Helmets should be buckled. Some people use a plastic chin strap which also serves as a chin protector. Others wear plastic guards across their mouths. These may seem foolish, but you can have debris thrown into your face by the rear wheels of the car or truck ahead of you. Here again, these things are not always needed if you have either a windshield or a fairing. Your helmet should fit snugly. After it is on your head and showroom, place your hands on both sides of your head and twist the helmet, holding your head straight. If it goes off more than three or four degrees it is too loose. In purchasing a helmet, buy one as tight as you can get it without pressure or strain in any part of your head. The best way to say it is "snug." The helmets should be of the type that offers full protection around the neck and to the front of the jawline. Half helmets or helmets with a skull shell and leather ear- and neckpieces not only don't offer as much protection, but could very well be the cause of a more serious injury in an accident. Helmet color deserves a mention. There are many very attractive multicolored helmets on the market today. They're certainly more attractive than the plain white one, but, if I have any influence on the rider at all, may I point out to you that the white helmet may be the only thing that a motorist would see at night other than your taillight? You need to be noticed; I've stressed this in all parts of this book. Poor visibility is easily the largest single cause of motorcycle accidents in the United States today. A helmet should be white and if I ever had my way, the helmets would be covered with a highly reflective material such as Scotchlite. Some states even require Scotchlite reflective tape on the helmet.

New types of goggles are coming out every day with anti-fog devices if you don't wish to wear face shields. These do fit over glasses and some of them fit under the helmet and some over. Look carefully the way the strap is attached to the goggles as this will indicate whether you wear the goggles over your helmet without letting in an air draft. People with narrow faces are going to find difficulty in getting a pair of goggles that will fit inside the outer limits of their helmet. If you get a helmet small enough and your goggles won't fit, you'll have to go to face shields. Face shields are safer than goggles. They can be quickly flipped up whereas trying to rip off goggles can occupy too many seconds during a blinding fog.

Any motorcyclist that travels long distances is going to need one of the new black-elastic ribbed kidney belts. Most motorcycles vibrate constantly because of the position in which a motorcyclist must seat himself on the bike in order to drive properly. The kidney belt is unobtrusive, it is worn under your shirt. It isn't bulky and it effectively reduces back strain. A must for the serious motorcyclist. Good-looking for your figure, too.

There are some "no-no's." Sneakers are one, dress shoes, another. These two do not give adequate ankle protection. Stay away from vinyl boots—especially the rear passenger, since one touch on the muffler and you have a melted sole or heel. Boots that are zippered up the side or rear are perfectly adequate. There is no need for all-weather protection such as the off-the-road enthusiast needs when he goes through a large stream. There is a good deal of puddling and splashing after rainstorms and boots can very quickly become saturated. Aside from the boots getting heavy, your feet also get wet unless the boots are leather and protected, as I mentioned at the beginning of the chapter, with neat's-foot oil. The soles should not be plain rubber or vinyl. They should preferably be ribbed or cut-up rubber or leather. Of the two, I suggest cut-up rubber.

This gives you a nonskid surface and something you can stab at a brake or shift lever without slipping off it. Also, when you come to a stop at a light or stop sign, you will find that your feet grip better.

The name of the game in long-distance driving or touring is comfort. It is very easily achieved with the proper outfits. Other costumes such as swimsuits, bikinis, casual shirts, jeans, and other cloth pants are invitations to serious injuries.

As to accessory clothes, socks should be 100 percent wool, even in the summer. They allow good breathing for the foot and the foot needs air and exercise. As in the army, you should bring extra pairs of clean socks and an extra pair of boots, as well as all outer and inner clothing.

If you are wearing leathers, a rain suit is a must. If you use a snowmobile suit, you can zip it on and ignore the rain suit. At the risk of being redundant, may I suggest you try and find a jump suit made of a white material for nighttime driving, preferably highly reflective or laced with Scotchlite tape. This will improve the motorist's awareness of you at night.

For those, such as myself, who like to ride below freezing, ski masks with the little holes cut out for the eyes and nose are very effective for keeping the chill wind off on a speedy drive on a turnpike. Even if you do frighten everybody in the passing automobiles, you will at least be comfortable.

Many riders wear a navy watch cap—a navy blue knitted affair—under their helmets in the winter for extra warmth. It is my feeling that, with a proper-rated helmet closely fitted and enclosing the ears, extra headgear under the helmet is not necessary.

Helmet, boots, and gloves are always useful no matter how short or how long the drive. These should be on your list as the minimum when you go out to ride.

Scarves are not recommended. If the rider wears one, the passenger gets whipped. If the passenger wears one, it could pull the passenger back because of the whipping action when a scarf gets loose. They have been known to blow in front of a rider's face and to blind him. If they are worn by those of us who use them in the winter, they are wrapped around securely and placed inside of the jacket.

Personal safety also includes a few rules and regulations such as: Don't ever read or try to do something when you drive. That includes smoking. Many motorcyclists have been

This picture shows you things not to do, like driving without a helmet and trying to read a magazine while driving.

burned severely or distracted by ashes blowing into their eyes, which may cause an accident. It is difficult at times on long-distance driving to sit in one position; for this reason, many cyclists wiggle to what I call "half positions." Half of your butt is twisted to the right and another time twisted to the left. Your feet can sometimes be elevated, especially if you have safety bars with an extra set of pegs to rest your feet, providing you have the right type of highway ahead of you.

If you feel tired it is best to stop and walk around and get a little exercise or sit down and take a quick nap. Everything pointed out for the driver applies also to the passenger. There is a note I would like to add here. Some women don't like to put their arms around the driver to hold on. Perhaps they think it is a mark of intimacy that they don't feel for the person they are riding with. This may be, but it is a very poor practice to use either no hands or to put your hands on the little handles that are behind you. With your hands behind you, you might go into a backward somersault, should your rider inadvertently jerk out in first gear.

Secondly, with a distance between the rider and the passenger, the motorcycle is out of balance and you cannot "feel" the leaning in and out of turns. From the rider's point of view, he begins to wobble as the weight gets too far back of the rear wheel and he is unable to maneuver as efficiently as with the weight in one solid mass together.

This isn't a plea for togetherness as much as it is a plea for good safety practices. Personal safety of the rider and passenger requires a smooth, well-coordinated passenger who doesn't anticipate the turn ahead of the driver, but leans with him. It is a real joy to have a passenger on the back who knows how to handle his or her end. Conversely, one of the biggest horror shows is to ride with somebody who fights you at every turn.

Some people who have toured for years have found that they can actually go to sleep on the back of the rider without falling off. Believe me, if you are tired enough, you would do the same and you will stay there.

It is always a good idea to carry things such as apples and a thermos of coffee on extremely long trips. More so than in an automobile. The constant vibration and the droning of mile after mile in one position have a hypnotic effect on both rider and passenger. Frequent stops along the highway are a must. Trips should be planned so that there is no pressure to make a special schedule.

Those of us who do a lot of winter driving use a turtle-neck "dickey" that slips over the head and covers the throat and upper chest and fits inside the shirt or jacket.

There are many special types of gloves for the subzero enthusiast. Eddie Bauer in Seattle, Washington, makes a pair of ski mitts for about $16.95. They are made of special down and give your hands extra protection.

Your knees get cold quicker than your legs or toes, and the knee protection made by Enduro Products in Milford,

Connecticut, is almost a must for the winter buff.

Being in good physical condition is a must for anyone who rides long distances. A tremendous amount of fresh air tires you quickly. Long distances in cramped saddle positions are enervating. Frequent stops are the rule of the road. Your personal safety requires that you never drive when you are tired.

This picture shows a ski mask worn under a helmet and heavy winter driving mitts. The advantage of the ski mask is that it fills all the air spaces between the head or face and the helmet. This enables the driver to use his motorcycle in temperatures down to about 20° in the winter.

8

Advanced Riding Techniques

THERE are drivers and then there are racing drivers. There are pilots and there are professional drivers. You might think looking at a motorcycle on the highway that there isn't much difference between one motorcyclist and another as far as technique is concerned. To a degree this is true. After all, the motorcycle is a mechanical contrivance and if the cyclist is an expert at smooth shifting and smooth braking, you'd be hard put to it to determine whether he was what you'd call an expert road rider.

To the discerning eye, there are differences. If you look very very carefully, you can determine who's the professional and who's the amateur.

Assuming you've watched a few people ride motorcycles, you know that if a rider blasts off from the motorcycle dealer's parking lot, he's a showoff. Mark him down one. If he changes his muffler to an open pipe for the noise effect, you know he's immature. Mark him down again. If he doesn't have a helmet on you know he's no pro. If he's chopped his bike and uses it for shows, he's a connoisseur, but if he uses it on the road, he's driving a bomb.

If he's in traffic and weaves in and out, mark him down. If he sneaks up inside a lane of cars or to the right of a lane of cars, mark him down again. If he rides double, that is, motorcycle side by side with another motorcycle in the same lane, once again put him down.

If he wheelies along the street or makes a doughnut in the parking lot, he's simply not emotionally mature enough to be allowed to drive a motorcycle.

Now there are qualifiers to all of this. One is if he's got a woods machine and he's playing around in his parking lot or a dealer's parking lot making doughnuts or wheelies. This is just part of the fun so long as it doesn't interfere with other people who come to the dealer's. Woods machines are set up for this sort of thing, so you have to determine what type of cycle he has. But in general all of the above is true.

So how do you tell the advanced rider and how can you become a professional motorcyclist?

Assuming you have already learned to drive as outlined in chapter 4 and have had some experience in traffic, it's now time to learn some of the advanced riding techniques that professionals use. First understand that there are six positions in an accident:

1. Head-on ⎫
2. Tail-on ⎬ (Principal positions)
3. Collision/car turning left
4. Collision/oncoming car drifting over center line
5. Intersection collisions
6. Passed/being passed

These six positions are the only ways that you can have an accident involving another vehicle. If you're aware of them, you have a point in your favor.

1. *Head-on.* The head-on is listed as one of the principal causes of or principal positions in an accident. This usually occurs on a two-lane road where somebody crosses the line and

is similar to number 4. You should plan evasive action. You should be prepared and have programmed in your mind exactly what you think you'd do if a head-on situation arose. Can you make a quick turn to the right to avoid a head-on? If you made a quick turn to the left, would this bring you in a position that would jeopardize your safety in relationship to other cars behind the one about to hit you head-on? Should you dive the bike? Should you dump it on the left and let it slide on the crash bars into a head-on situation? One of these evasive actions is the right one, but which depends on the situation. Each of the evasive actions outlined above should be programmed into your mind and you should be thinking about them from time to time, sort of "war gaming" what you would do if a situation arose.

2. *Tail-on*. The evasive action here is first to develop the habit of constantly checking both left and right rearview mirrors. When you find you're being tailgated, try to flash your brake light very gently to see if this slows down the tailgater. If it doesn't and you feel you're not getting enough space between you and the tailgater, the immediate and best way out of that situation is to drift over to the right of your lane and give him a passing signal. It may hurt your pride to let him pass, but it will avoid a very dangerous situation. If a tailgater just touches your bike, it'll throw you off balance and you will probably overturn. So there are two evasive actions there, constant looking in the mirror to be aware of a situation and allowing the tailgater to pass if you can't get him to back off.

3. *Collision/car turning left*. Usually there is an indication when a car starts to turn left in front of you. You can take evasive action by checking the front wheels of the car ahead of you at all times. In general, your attention can be called when he is approximately opposite an intersection or a side road. Usually a driver telegraphs his intention even if he doesn't give you directional signals or hand signals. An almost imperceptible slowing down, a slight cocking of the wheels to the left. Now remember you're riding to the left of center in your own lane. Another exceptionally fine way to avoid this situation is to keep plenty of distance between you and the car ahead of you. This applies to any situation. I well realize that leaving big spaces or gaps allows another car to drift over in front of you and between you and the car ahead.

This is a situation you're going to have to live with.

4. *Collision/oncoming car drifting over center line.* These drifters usually come on at night, but they can come on during the day. Somebody's not paying attention and this is the key to your evasion action. They're either asleep or they've been mesmerized by the road and don't understand what's going on, or their attention is distracted inside the car. You should be prepared for evasive action generally to the right, so you should be checking your right rearview mirror to see what is behind you on the right. Move to the right out of the passing lane into the driving lane. If you are already in the driving lane, see what your safety options are. There are situations where you can accelerate out of danger. This, of course, is a matter of judgment and can only be determined at the exact moment of your awareness of the situation, but you can be prepared for that oncoming car drifting over.

5. *Intersection collisions.* These are most dangerous for two reasons. One is the driver on your right or left is not usually aware of you. This is that psychological factor we spoke of earlier. The other is he may just plain be arrogant and feel that you have no right on the highway and, therefore, he will go ahead of you. In general, drivers tend to alternate across an intersection when there is a line of vehicles backed up behind each stop sign. This does not always take place when a motorcycle is one of those involved. Usually the one on the right is the one to look out for.

Your evasive action might be to be able to turn to the left, but this would place you in jeopardy with oncoming traffic. Turning to the right would force you to turn into the driver crossing from the right, and this generally is what has happened in this type of accident. Speeding up is playing Russian roulette with a motorcycle and a car and it doesn't work in this situation. One of the other evasive actions is the slide, the left slide, since neither vehicle is going very fast at this time.

When approaching an intersection be very careful to keep your eye out to both the right and the left to see who's coming up to the stop sign and whether or not they pay attention to it and, if they do stop, whether or not they start up again.

6. *Passed/being passed.* These are extremely dangerous. Passing requires that you give good signals to the driver behind that you intend to pull out and pass. If possible, you should have your light on at all times, and in all of the six

positions of an accident, make liberal use of directional signals and hand signals in combination. Signal the driver ahead of you either by flashing your headlight, using your horn, or a combination of both. Make certain that he sees you in his rear-view mirror. You can look into his rearview mirror and tell whether or not he sees you. If you can see his face, even though it's indistinct, and you are keeping your distance, you should be able to tell whether the driver ahead has his head in position to see you. Whatever you do, don't travel in a blind spot. Speed up. Having memorized part 375, you know exactly how many feet it takes you to make a high-speed pass. After checking the traffic behind you, pull out and make your pass positively, firmly, and at speed, but control your speed, making certain that you have room enough to pull back in. Anticipate that the driver you are passing will speed up as an aggressive movement on his part. If he is an emotionally adjusted person, he won't speed up. He might even slow down to give you a better opportunity to pull in. Make sure you have sufficient room to pull in way ahead of him or don't attempt to pass. Most accidents have happened because the cyclist has over-estimated his ability. He has a low-powered bike or he has a passenger and too much luggage on the back and can't pass in time, so he gets trapped out in the middle. Thinking that he isn't as bulky as the car and he should therefore be able to skin through isn't good enough. It certainly isn't defensive driving and it isn't safe. Practice those high-speed passes.

When you're being passed, stay to the left of center of your lane. Do not let the driver force you to the right-hand side of your lane so that he can use your lane as his passing lane. He must make his passing period in the opposite lane or passing lane. You may signal your understanding of his intention by looking in your rearview mirror: he'll see you looking in the mirror at him.

It is not, I repeat, a good practice to pull over to the right half of your lane and let him use your lane. You'll be forced off the road if he has misjudged his passing time. However, pulling over in the right side of your lane is your defensive maneuver in the event something goes wrong with his passing. It's best to drop back and give him plenty of room. It's only common courtesy if he's trapped out there to pull over and let him in. It's foolish pride for those who feel that it serves him right.

Airplane pilots have used checklists for years. A motorcyclist has six additional problems other than the six positions for an accident. These are conditions, and these conditions affect everything about his driving technique. We should be aware of them, we should understand them, and we should be prepared to take evasive action in the event of adverse conditions.

1. Light
2. Weather
3. Road condition or expected condition
4. Traffic condition or expected condition
5. Vehicle condition
6. Physical condition

1. *Light.* If you know you're going to be out after dark, you should check your lights, check your battery. Make sure you have no burned-out bulbs and make sure that you have sufficient illumination to see and to be seen.

2. *Weather.* Advanced weather reports for extended touring are a must. You should expect rain. Be prepared with rain suits. Be certain to have a windshield cut low enough to look over. Be certain that you have a flip shield on your helmet and changes of clothing.

3. *Road condition or expected conditions.* If you plan your route well, you know what type of road you'll be driving over. Plan emergency and rain stops. Analyze your entire route and estimate what you might need or what type of road condition you can expect. Be especially careful of construction areas.

4. *Traffic condition or expected conditions.* Massive traffic, such as in and out of metropolitan areas on summer weekends —outgoing on Fridays and returns on Sunday nights on interstates and freeways—can give you bumper-to-bumper traffic that can be extremely dangerous. There's a great temptation to travel up between lanes or run along the outside. Both are illegal maneuvers. Try to plan your trips in such a way that you can go back home in the early hours of the morning when there's good daylight, it's cool, and the traffic is at its lightest. Don't travel late at night. Big trailers can run you down. The lighting is inadequate, and on superhighways, turnpikes, and

the like, a speed of 70 mph is common. Unless you can sustain such a speed, don't mix with that kind of traffic.

5. *Vehicle condition.* The condition of your vehicle in road riding must be one of the top considerations. The chain must be properly adjusted and oiled. That's number one. Have an adequate or full amount of gas, proper oil, and check all your bulbs and switches. Make sure that your tire pressure is at the proper level and that tires are not worn or have any abrasions in them. Check all bolts for tightness.

6. *Physical condition.* You can't dope off on the highway. You've got to be in exceptionally fine physical condition. This means plenty of rest before a trip. It means a healthy run or other type of exercise if it's at all possible just before you go on long road rides. Break up your hours with ten-minute rest periods. Pull off alongside the highway, then walk for a bit and stretch your legs. You can sustain a long trip. I've done it up to ten hours by taking five minutes out of every hour or to the nearest hour, pulling off the highway, and running in place to get my circulation going. Plan your trips so you're not riding into the sun or at least to a minimum extent. That summer sun can bore a hole right into your brain. If you drive a lot in the winter as I do, you're going to find yourself getting very cold. You must get off that bike more frequently, maybe every 30 minutes, and get the blood circulating. Eyestrain is one of the biggest problems in long touring. I find face shields have glare, so I usually change to goggles with colored lenses but only during sunny daylight hours. Yellow, amber, and other colored lenses have a way of making everything look rosy, dilating your eyes and causing eyestrain.

So these are six conditions that must be thought about and planned for prior to the trip. The professional road rider makes a checklist of these six conditions and the six positions of an accident and attempts to anticipate any and all situations.

Remember that you're "pilot in command." This means you have the responsibility of the safety and comfort of your passenger, therefore, it behooves you to examine your passenger's kit to see that he or she has everything that is needed for the trip. Make a checklist and go over every single item. Passengers often act as navigators. It's best to acquaint them with the six trip conditions and the six accident positions.

Explain your evasion techniques and explain your preparation for the six conditions.

Dropping your bike. I don't recommend practicing this, but during the war, I taught motorcycling for a while at the Armored Force Center at Fort Knox, Kentucky, and we were taught to lay those bikes down on the left side. They were all equipped with safety bars, but the experience of purposely dumping a bike at 30 mph was quite something. The first time especially it was a little bit hairy. The training stood me in good stead because for many years I have been able to lay a bike down. Not too many safety books are going to mention this, and I am sure motorcycle manufacturers aren't. Once again I am going to take the writer's prerogative and tell you to lay that bike down. Every once in a while you can avoid extensive injury to yourself by dropping it.

Dropping is a technique, and anybody who has had some experience in the woods has already dropped his bike. Maybe he didn't intend to do so, but he has and he would probably approach a highway drop without as much trepidation as you would. The secret of dropping a bike quickly is to cause a sideways skid by cocking your handlebar slightly to the right and leaning to the left and giving sudden, almost locked-up, right-foot brake. No front brake! This will drop it.

I rounded a corner once in Suffern, New York, about 30 years ago, and right in front of me was a stalled car. Luckily I was making a left turn. It was at night, I was fresh out of the army, and without even thinking I just dumped her. We slid along on that left safety bar and went right up to the car. I am positive if I had hit him straight up he would have dented in my face. As it was, I had a badly mangled bike and some skin off my left side. Of course, if you have a passenger in this type of situation the best thing is full brakes, without lockup. Use your rear foot brake a little bit ahead of the application of the front brake and in a straight-up configuration. Brace your arms, because that passenger's weight is going to come up on you about three "Gs."

9

Riding with a Passenger

THE addition of 100 to 150 pounds of weight on the back of your motorcycle does change some of the riding characteristics of the bike. The main effort should be to keep the center of gravity as close to you as possible. Any passenger should ride with his hands on your waist and as close to you as possible. If the rider follows your lead, it is very much like a dance. When you lean, the passenger leans, and after a while there will be no perceptible difference between the movements of the two of you. This means "you are dancing" in unison. A good rider makes motorcycling a pleasure, and a poor rider makes it a chore and very tiring.

Caution your passenger to leave his or her feet on the foot pegs at all times—even when you come to a stop. Their attempts to help you balance the machine will only interfere. It is easier for you to balance the machine with weight properly distributed and the feet of the passenger on the pegs. To attempt to help you to balance the machine at a stoplight will cause them to unconsciously fight your control of the machine.

Passengers get tired too and want to shift their weight. When they do this, it should be on a straight stretch at a time when here is an opportunity for you to change positions and for you and the rider to balance out the shift.

The passenger should be wearing a three-quarter or full helmet. Years ago, half helmets were devised with all sorts of fancy ribbons for the ladies to wear. This was a compromise with safety in the name of fashion. *There are no compromises with safety.* A well-fitted full or three-quarter helmet is required for the passenger as much as it is for yourself. Goggles are still necessary as well as protective clothing as outlined in the previous chapter. Warmth is not quite as much of a problem because the passenger can ride close to you and be shielded from wind by your body. Even to the point of following the contours of your legs and upper legs.

A good passenger likes to see what is going on rather than just looking sideways at scenery flashing by. They will often peer around your right side or left side to get a glimpse of what is going on ahead. With a good rider, this doesn't materially affect your balance because the passenger tends to peer around you without moving his body. If a passenger shifts the weight materially, suggest that he pick one or the other side and alternate them from time to time, but not every minute or two because this does cause you to shift your balance control.

Some couples lock a belt around both of them. Others use the large belts with handles that are becoming popular. The belt is around the driver and the handles are for the passenger. Old-timers just hang on around the waist. After you have ridden with someone for a while, you get to know the feel of how he drives and the rider can balance without even holding on. I don't suggest that though.

Passengers on small bikes pose a problem. They have to put their heels on the pegs pointing their heels out in order to give you shifting and braking room. Since you have to sit forward, you'll find it difficult to keep your heels on the pegs in order to get the feel of shifting and braking. Suggest to these passengers that they sit as far back as they can and, if their rear pegs are close to the front ones, have them cock their toes out using just their heels. This helps during periods of city traffic or congested areas where you have to shift back and forth.

Out in the country you can assume more comfortable positions with your feet.

Obviously, any acrobatic antics are out. Although I have seen passengers bouncing up and down on the rear, they would not realize that they were beyond the rear axle and could very easily cause a backflip.

As I mentioned in a previous chapter, sleeping on the back has been done. Some very long distance tourists use a sissy bar packed with sleeping bags and this makes a comfortable backrest. It is more dangerous to sleep leaning back than it is leaning forward.

When children are passengers, although they have less weight, they are apt to be squirmy and of course they can't see over Daddy's shoulders and sometimes they can't see around them. This is one of those things that has to be accepted. The tendency to want to put the child up in front of you up on the gas tank is asking for trouble for any long-distance ride. It is a great way to go a short distance around the driveway or a parking lot in order to give a youngster a taste or feel of riding on a motorcycle. But for anything beyond this, you might try a safety belt wrapped around the two of you if you insist on putting a young child up in front of you. Most safety pamphlets and books say that children should ride behind and, if they are too young to ride behind, they shouldn't be on the bike at all. It sounds like good advice, but I know myself. I have ridden a number of kids up on the tank in front of me and, by using a big belt and strapping them to me, I have felt that they were perfectly safe for their indoctrination ride, but certainly not for long-distance touring.

Whenever riding with a passenger, especially a neophyte, check him out as to what's hot and what isn't and what he can step on and can't. Be sure the passenger's heels don't dig back into the spokes. There is nothing like shredded boot to mar an otherwise happy picnic day. Most big motorcycles have big chain guards so there isn't much chance of getting a foot caught in that area. The biggest problem, as I mentioned once before, is burning the passenger's boots on the mufflers.

Passenger carrying is fun. Long-distance touring means someone to share your joys as well as your tribulations. There is a big responsibility involved, so make sure you take that responsibility seriously. Check your insurance and make sure you have passenger liability. In the event of an accident, you could be causing both yourself and your passenger irreparable harm.

10

Riding at Night

Obviously the biggest problem in night driving is your ability to see and be seen. The most dangerous part of night driving is twilight. It is at this time, when your eyes are becoming adjusted to night driving, that you see the least.

Night driving requires a sturdy headlight in good working order. Constantly check it. If you are the type of person who drives out knowing you might come back after dark, make certain that the headlight and the taillight are working and working well, also that your battery is up to snuff. Check your high and low beams to see that they are working adequately. If they are in series, separate them so they are in parallel. Some of the modern big touring bikes have automatic switchovers. If one beam goes out, the other cuts in. *This is a tremendous safety factor.* It is something to think about when buying. Try for a 12 volt instead of a 6 volt and get yourself a big front-end lamp—if you are going to do any night driving at all. Federal laws say you should be able to see an object in the road at 500 feet. If that object is a white truck you will obviously see it, but if it is a block of wood, animal, or a piece of tire, you are going to need that extra lighting. Check your lights and measure the distance you can see with your lights and never overreach it. When you get behind a car, it is best to use your low beams. Just because you have one headlight doesn't mean you won't blind the truck or car in front of you. Depth perception is difficult at night. Avoid tailgating and remember the 40-foot rule. Give yourself 40 feet for each 10 miles an hour of speed. This distance kept properly will enable you to react to the movements of the driver ahead—if he brakes to a sudden stop.

I previously mentioned that you should set your bike up, engine running, motor on, give it a 2100 rpm, then have someone else pace out the distance of 500 feet. Just tell them to take "300 giant steps forward." Naturally you can see him going out there all the way so it is a little unfair, but have him put a block of wood in the highway and see if you can see it. If you find you have light problems, and most everybody does, you either drive slower at night or you get yourself some quartz-iodide lights and give yourself that extra margin of safety. Remember in some states these lights are illegal so you may have to put covers over them. Most of them come with covers for that purpose. Covers are a good idea in the daytime anyway. They prevent stone, rocks, and other obstacles from breaking them.

In some states, and it may soon be a law in most of them, you are going to have to ride with your headlight on anyway. So, when you are buying a bike, think of the electrics. Find out from other riders how reliable they are and take a good look at that headlight. Some of the new big bikes have sealed-beam headlights and they are every bit as good as those on a car. That isn't saying too much though. In this country they don't allow you to have really good lighting; they are afraid of your blinding another driver.

Night driving does impose responsibilities for having clean windshields, as I pointed out, and also a very clean and

This motorcyclist pulling out in front of a car at night is nearly invisible, even in the glare of car lights 5 feet away. The large aluminum engine is the only source of reflectance.

This photograph is taken much later at night, but notice the difference in the high-reflectance, il-luminized suit that this driver is wearing. This motorcycle suit is called a Full-Bore. It's water repellent, lined with foam insulation, and, at the moment, it is the best and the safest motorcycle suit that can be worn. It comes in two pieces.

This is all that's visible of the rider at 25 feet.

At approximately 25 feet, late at night, notice the difference in visibility.

130

At 50 feet he all but disappears. Had he worn a highly reflective riding suit not only would he be visible, but identifiable.

The motorcyclist is at 100 feet, the cars are at 500 feet. I have lightened the print somewhat to show the relationship between the oncoming cars, which even at this distance are identifiable, and the cylist and my car.

Here, the motorcyclist is at 100 feet wearing a highly reflective suit. This is taken on a different night, and much later at night. Notice there is no sky visible. The motorcyclist is identifiable and visible.

unscratched goggle or face shield. A light from an oncoming driver can reflect in your lens and defract, scattering the rays and causing "flare" that will momentarily blind you. This is one of the two biggest dangers. The other is lack of adequate headlighting.

When you round a curve on a country road at night, remember that your lamp shines off into the bushes or, at the very best, it follows the shoulder of the road. Once again, investigate a secondary quartz light, maybe canted so that it flares out in front of you for about 100 yards. This could be put on a spring return button switch and you can press it momentarily when you need that extra light.

One of the big complaints about visibility or lack of it is that a single light destroys the ability of the driver of the car to estimate the distance of the oncoming vehicle, in this case a motorcycle. Two lights allow you to estimate distance; one offers no opportunity for accurate judgment.

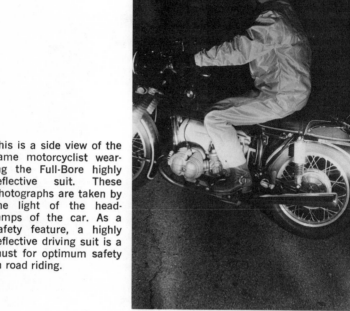

This is a side view of the same motorcyclist wearing the Full-Bore highly reflective suit. These photographs are taken by the light of the head-lamps of the car. As a safety feature, a highly reflective driving suit is a must for optimum safety in road riding.

Weight has always been a problem with motorcycles. Everybody seems to want the lightest bike he can get. When I go touring, I don't care how much my bike weighs (within limits). I definitely need some things and one is a good battery. Compare the plate and ampere/hour rating for the different bikes you contemplate buying. You might ask the dealer if there is any chance of substituting a heavy-duty one if you are going to do a lot of night driving.

Taillights and directional signals are of paramount importance at night. You are almost invisible. You still have that same syndrome I mentioned in one of the earlier chapters, of the driver's not "seeing" you. If he creeps up behind you, he generally does see you. This is why some motorcyclists will always wear a white helmet whether or not it matches the color of the tank and fenders. Some states require Scotchlite; it is a highly reflective plastic, self-adhesive. Scotchlite strips are used on highway guard posts in some states, and in other states they are required on your helmet. They are a good idea. They alert the driver behind you that there is something up ahead from a greater distance than the driver can see your vehicle.

Extra reflectors on your taillight assembly are always welcome as long as they don't confuse the issue when the brake lights come on.

Light-colored clothing is always worn at night. It makes you much more visible and, for that matter, a white bike with a white outfit with white helmet would be the most visible of all at night.

Make sure your face shields are flip-up as I mentioned in a previous chapter.

The road seems to mesmerize drivers at night. Following the yellow center line (being changed from white) will put you to sleep. Try to look out ahead with your eyes along your beam. This would be about three-quarters of the distance of your beam including the end of the beam and the top of your peripheral vision.

Should you have a lot of gaudy lights on your dash, install a rheostat and cut them down or ask a good mechanic to put a resistor in series so that the bulbs dim down to where they are just visible.

Another caution about night driving. If you are driving in unfamiliar territory and you don't know what the land is like, your roadway could turn from asphalt to concrete to steel grating, to sand or almost anything. You must be prepared for each and every one of these in unfamiliar areas. Drive defensively as if you knew they existed in front of you.

When making turns at night on secondary roads or country roads, I ride almost to the center of the road. The edges have too much loose sand, leaves, dirt, and debris. (There are still litterers, you know.) It is not as dangerous as it sounds because you can see the headlights of an oncoming car and move over if necessary long before he gets to you.

Our little furry friends are out at night, too. Please try not to hit them. I hate hitting an animal; I have killed them, but never intentionally. I have felt bad about it each time, but it is better to hit one than it is to take evasive action. Evasive action could mean an accident, with damage to you and your bike. You don't have the time you have in daylight. The best thing to do is to keep going unless the animal is very, very large, like a deer, cow, horse, or bear. But the small animals I am afraid you will have to hit rather than swerve and try to avoid them.

Brer fox could cause an accident. Be wary of animals, blocks of wood, strips of rubber tire from trucks on the highway.

Notice the fox in the leaves alongside the front wheel. A big problem with lighting on motorcycles is that they don't show these things at night.

11

Rain and Snow Riding

ANYBODY who rides a road bike for any appreciable period of time is going to encounter rain. You simply can't avoid getting wet sometime. Riding a motorcycle in the rain is a skill and like any other skill it can be learned. One of the best teachers is experience. Before you get that experience, if you have a knowledge of what to expect, what the driving conditions are, and what you can do about it, then you can prevent a lot of grief and make it actually enjoyable.

The difference between rain on the road and none is a thin film of water between that portion of your tires that touches the road and the road itself. Rain in itself is not the problem. The first problem arises from what happens when the first shower or heavy rain hits a well-traveled road.

138

Prior to the shower, many vehicles, cars, trucks, and so on, have been driving over the roadway leaving a thin film of oil, grease, and carbon solids. The majority of these are in the center of the lane and are easily visible. However, the entire roadway has a film of grease and oil on it. As you know from your high school chemistry, oil and water do not mix and oil rises. When it rains, the oil rises to the surface causing a very slick or slippery condition. The rain flushes out all the oil that has seeped down into the crevices and cracks in the road. A light shower is the most dangerous, because it is wet enough to float the oil and wet enough to create an oil slick that is just like glare ice.

If the rain is a hard one, you should stop. If you are on a parkway, pull off under a bridge or if you are on a secondary road, pull off into the nearest diner and have a cup of coffee. The chances are that this oil slick will be washed away, but it takes at least half an hour in a heavy rain. Now, this time is a guess and it is relative to a lot of conditions such as how dry the weather has been in this part of the country before the rain. If it has been raining on and off for three or four days, you can safely get back on that road within fifteen or twenty minutes or as soon as the heavy rain stops. You will find now your problem will be visibility, which we will go into later. If it has been a long time since this road has had water on it, there will be some slick.

Park under a bridge when it begins to rain, the first 30 minutes anyway. This gives the rain a chance to raise the oil and wash it away. The most dangerous time to ride is during this first period.

I suggest that you go out and look at it. It won't hurt to get down on your haunches and take a good look at it. Just don't get clipped by a car. Notice the multicolored wavery lines of oil floating on top of the puddles and watch what happens when the droplets hit. Some roads get slicker than others. Macadam is not as bad as concrete. Dirt roads just tend to muddy up, causing another set of problems. We will assume that you are on a road bike and you are touring, so we will stick pretty close to the problems of paved roads.

As I said before, if the rain is coming down hard, there is not much you can do about it anyway so it is best to get off the road. I worked as a flight instructor for over twenty years, and, without a doubt, the biggest single cause of accidents in commercial or general aviation today is "pushing weather." Students, private pilots, commercial students, they have to get home or they have to get back for either economic reasons or for some engagement or work, and they will push the weather. This means they will take chances flying into weather they don't belong in.

In motorcycling and especially touring, one should be prepared to stop, relax, and enjoy whatever life brings you. If you are in a summer rainstorm, you can expect it will pass over in a short while. There are certain rains that are lasting. Weather reports are very handy before beginning a day's touring, but don't be afraid to pull over and stop. Don't take chances.

When you drive in the rain there are things you can do to lessen the danger and to solve the problems, and this applies to snow just as well as it does to rain.

Rule No. 1. Slow down. Above 40 mph your motorcycle starts to "plane." You are what we call "up on the step" in seaplane flying or "skiing." This means you have lost *traction.* So, stay below 40 mph and you will find the rain on your windshield or fairing and your face shield won't be quite as stinging and your visibility will be better as well.

Rule No. 2. Don't do any sharp braking. This is why in the chapter on Maintenance, you learned to pay particular attention to how your brakes grab. This is another good reason why disc brakes are better than drum brakes; they don't grab and they don't fade. A disc brake allows good, solid, even pressure without locking up or jerking. Although, there is not that much danger even with drum brakes. Apply smooth, even application and start with the rear brake ever so slightly ahead of the front. But remember that it is the rear that skids, so more reliance is going to be placed on the front brake. Remember, as you apply your front brake you are also locking up your steering. But that is good, you aren't going to do that much steering anyway. You want to remain upright. This means defensive driving with more attention paid when pulling up behind a car, the distance ahead of the car in back of you, passing, and deceleration, and smooth, even application of the throttle and maintaining distance between vehicles in front of you. Don't let that clutch out with a jerk. Between this and the previous rule, it should give you some thoughts on how to conduct your pretrip maintenance. Think about how important it is to have a smooth clutch, smooth braking. What you did at home will show up out on the road maybe 200 miles away.

Rule No. 3. Turn your lights on. This would probably be first if you went out into the rain, but if you are caught out in the rain, put it in this position. Your lights will give better visibility to other drivers both oncoming and the drivers ahead of you and behind you. They will see you and know you are there. They appreciate the fact that you are on a slippery surface. Another good reason for pretrip maintenance, battery, generator, alternator, voltage regulator, diodes, all in good working order. Spare bulbs are a must on a trip.

Rule No. 4. Make all turns upright. Driving in the rain is no place for leaning into a turn. If you are going slow enough, and you should be, you can drive around a turn. If it is a sharp one, a slow, easy turn is a must.

Rule No. 5. Avoid all puddles. They could be covering potholes. Even if they aren't covering a hole, splashing will only serve to soak your lower leg and your feet. Another good reason for splash guards on your lower fender or knee guards in the winter.

Rule No. 6. Look out for metal in the roadway, such as metal grates, railroad tracks, sewer covers, manhole covers: all of these are superslick. If railroad tracks are at an angle to the direction of your travel, cross them at 90° to the track. Under no circumstances must you get caught in a rail. Here is another good reason for not tailgating. A driver comes to a

142

This type of sewer cover is most dangerous in wet weather, such as rain or snow, when it becomes extremely slippery. These and other manholes should be avoided in inclement weather.

Turning a corner on wet pavement. This type, which is an entrance ramp to an Interstate, is supposed to be the best kind of highway in the United States. Use very little lean to turn. All turns on wet pavement are made slowly and upright.

Approach the railing in gear, at a moderate speed, but not under heavy load; you could cause skidding.

Railroad tracks should be crossed exactly perpendicular. Notice the rut or groove of the near rail. Anyone attempting to cross these at less than 90° could be flipped.

light or a stop sign and you don't see that he is crossing a manhole cover until you are on it. Braking and acceleration on these things is impossible. Avoid them like the plague.

There are many steel-grating bridges in the United States. These bridges cause the motorcycle to wobble when you cross. The best way to cross is to ride "loose." When wet, they're covered with exhaust fumes and oil and very slippery. Try not to be nervous. Go over without excessive braking or acceleration.

>

The rider is left of center in his lane, the correct position. The center of the lane is covered with oil and slick as a whistle. Passing on the highway is doubly dangerous and not recommended unless the overtaken vehicle is moving very slowly.

Rule No. 7. Don't ride in the center of your lane. Ride in the worn area to the left of center. If you feel traffic is going to be passing you, use the right half of your lane. However, this usually invites passing. If you are anticipating the possibility that you may stop or get out of the rain, this is the part of the lane you should be in and ready to pull off at a moment's notice.

Shows the correct height for cutting a windshield. At 30 mph, the airflow goes over the top of the driver's helmet. The purpose of cutting the windshield lower than the eye level is so that you can see in driving rain and snow, or on those occasions, usually in the fall and spring, when you drive into a valley and your windshield fogs up. You must be able to see over your windshield; you certainly won't be able to see through it.

This rider is riding in the rain, wearing a rain suit but he forgot his boots, which means he will have wet feet. The visor, although correct in that it is a flip-up type, won't do him much good. He really needs a windshield or a fairing for continued driving in the rain. Note the "contact patch" (the area of contact with the road). His traction in the rain is about 6 inches in the front and 8 inches in the rear by about 2 inches in width. For prolonged riding in the rain he should drop his tire pressure from 25 to 18 pounds. This would increase his traction and hence give him better stability in rain.

Rule No. 8. Keep your distance. Every truck or automobile throws large swirling sprays of rain, mist, snow, and particles of sand and dirt. You haven't a windshield wiper on that windshield or fairing or on your visor. Good protection on these plastic items requires a heavy coat of LCI Anti-Fog Spray. Keep those windshields clean. Face shields too must be spotlessly clean. As soon as you are in this wet driving situation, they are going to get loaded with a muddy spray, so stay as far behind the vehicle ahead as you can. When your rearview mirror tells you that a car or truck is going to pass you, anticipate the spray. Be prepared. Look ahead on the road to see that there are no obstacles until you have a chance to regain your vision fully.

Rule No. 9. I am sure you have heard of "psyching." Racers psych each other out. You don't have to be a professional race driver in order to use psyching. Most people psych themselves. This is a form of fear that clutches at the heart: apprehension and inability to utilize skill and training. If you tense up in a situation like this, you are not going to do your best driving. Try and play it loose and calm and take everything as it comes. Above all—be prepared. Be relaxed as best you can on a motorcycle. Stiffening up isn't going to help you and your mind has got to be clear. It is not all that dangerous, take everything step by step. This entire chapter should be committed to memory. The key to any kind of successful safe motorcycling is in preparation, but you must anticipate each of the events that may happen to you and psyching is one.

Enough of rules. The rules are there but not to frighten you. They are made because, while motorcycling is a magnificent sport, there are limitations to man and his machine. The people who get into trouble are those who exceed either their or the machine's limitations. Lack of man's or machine's preparation on a tour is a big factor.

All of the rules that we have laid down here apply to snow as well as rain, but should be followed with even more caution in snow. Snow could cover ice and it could cover wet leaves or dirty newspapers or other debris. All of these things are slick, and all of them are designed to destroy your traction. Snow also sticks, and if it sticks to your windshield it is time to stop.

It is assumed that you have put on your rain suit or your snowmobile suit as soon as it started to rain or snow. It is important that your tires are in good condition with plenty of tread. A bald tire invites a skid. Tire care requires proper inflation. See your instruction book for the proper pressure for your bike. Remember, it varies with weight.

Prolonged driving in the rain washes off the oil on your chain. Remember to reoil it periodically. Shaft-driven bikes haven't this problem.

Chain adjustment must be carefully considered in order to prevent "jerks" in acceleration and deceleration.

Remember, discretion is the better part of valor.

12

Riding in the Mountains and Desert

ANY time you move from one environment to another, a different set of circumstances comes into play. Also the need for a different set of skills. Desert and mountain riding don't involve any particularly different techniques from anything else that has been previously covered. However, there are a great many other considerations that must be reckoned with.

Just the word *desert* and the word *mountain* imply that your gas stops are few and far between. Motorcycle dealer shops where one might buy a tire or a tube are a great distance apart. This implies that greater consideration must be given to the care and feeding of the mechanical monster.

The Care and Feeding of the Rider. This too can become a problem. Water must be carried with you. Canteens are a

149

vital necessity. Warm clothing is a must for mountain and desert riding. You can quite easily be traveling after sundown in a mountainous area at 40°, when the daytime temperature on the same tour was 120°.

Such things as sunburn lotion suddenly become important. Parts of your skin should not be exposed to the sun's rays in desert riding. The constant wind, hot winds at that, will dry your skin out and make it feel like an old piece of leather. Good gauntlet-type gloves are a necessity for desert riding.

Blowing dust can sting, so the face must be covered and you may have to carry two face shields. One may be destroyed, so be prepared to buy a third.

I have driven in the desert, across country, and I have crossed the Mojave. At the time I wore a $3.00 face mask with sponge rubber, for wear over the nose and mouth, that I used to soak in my canteen. This face mask was bought at Sears and it is used by paint sprayers. It is the best $3.00 I have ever spent.

Crossing the desert in the daytime caused all sorts of hallucinations after the first 50 miles. A combination of heat waves rising on the long, never-ending road caused me to hallucinate, and after a while there was a tendency to become mesmerized. The hypnotic effect becomes very dangerous. You develop a sort of euphoria.

The desert roads are hot and, when I say *hot,* I mean 110° to 130°. When you stop, you better not have thin-soled sneakers on. Good boots are a must.

I served in North Africa for a short while and I was always impressed with the Bedouins. They wore lots of clothing and covered up all parts of their skin and the only part that was visible was the eyes. The loose robes acted as an insulation, trapping a layer of perspiration that evaporates and becomes a cool air insulator. This, of course, is the fundamental theory of refrigeration. The American soldiers were running around in shorts and rapidly drying out their natural skin oils, getting sunburned and eventually dehydrated. I learned my lesson from these natives, and since then I have always worn lots of clothes, especially in hot weather. It is only a matter of wearing loose clothing, preferably with a loose weave.

Your feet must be properly booted regardless of the temperature.

Constant temperature changes have a way of wearing the rider and his passenger down very quickly. Temperatures of 90° to 120° will enervate even the most stalwart rider. A long tour requires that you be in excellent physical condition. Thermotabs (salt) are a must!

Care and Feeding of the Machine. With constantly blowing sand and dirt, you just know you are going to adjust that chain every 100 miles and you have got to keep it lubricated. That means you must carry a chain lube with you plus a tube repair kit and a full and complete set of tools and one of the small, hand tire pumps.

Oil changes should be more frequent in desert riding. A prolonged tour through the desert—2000 or 3000 miles' worth of riding over a period of a week or two, indicates an oil change at least every 1000 miles.

The air filter must definitely be cleaned off or the filter replaced as dust conditions demand. Even 100 miles in a dusty, windy area could mean a change of air filters. Not to pay attention to this can only invite disaster. That air filter is designed to prevent particles of dirt and dust from entering the throat of the carburetor and getting into the cylinder. Once inside the cylinder, all kinds of problems will arise. A complete breakdown is not inconceivable. In desert riding, the air filter box should be checked nightly. If necessary it should be re-cleaned or replaced. Spare filters should be brought along. The throat of the carburetor should be coated with a thin film of Vaseline to trap any dirt particles that do get by. This should be replaced depending on the amount of dirt and dust that you encounter.

The chain must be adjusted a minimum of every 100 miles. It must be carefully checked for dryness.

Blowing dirt and dust get into every part of your bike. It even seeps in through your clothes. If possible, wash the bike at every campsite or stop. Just a quick rinse-off would help. Remember these rinse-offs take off some of your wheel-bearing grease as well as your chain oil, so relubricate liberally.

As I mentioned in the chapter on Maintenance, screw-drivers are not tire irons. Make sure you have made a dry run of changing your tire before you go on a tour. The desert is no place to get caught with a flat. A spare tube should be brought along.

Sudden squalls seem to be a welcome relief to the tedium of a long desert run.

The mountains usually mean cooler temperatures, but winding roads with an especially heavily loaded bike have a tendency to overheat your engine. The rarefied air will definitely alter your carburetion. This can be solved with a minor adjustment of the air-gas ratio. A simple screwdriver to your low-speed jet may improve performance. Don't fool with this unless you are an expert mechanic and know what you are doing. Your air filters won't get as dirty in mountain riding as in desert riding, but your chain will need just as much adjustment. Falling rocks, washed out roads, these are all common pitfalls of mountain riding. Some of the breathtaking scenery is worth every bit of the problems. Remote mountainous roads are usually small and sometimes one lane. Riding on the outside, looking down into a canyon can be a real hairy experience. If you have any vertigo problems, I suggest not traveling the mountains—or don't look!

High altitudes mean that both you and your machine are working for oxygen. Plan shorter runs if you make them through high mountain areas. Be careful of animal crossings at night. Many cyclists traveling in mountainous and desert areas try to do some driving after twilight to take advantage of the coolness of the evening. I don't recommend this type of driving, I have done both, but I find night driving much more dangerous than driving in the daytime during the heat.

Long before you enter the desert area, the entire bike should have been lubricated and especially the cables.

Motorcycle touring brings one a little closer to the countryside than does the automobile. Certainly it is easier to stop and enjoy a special view. I have ridden all over this country, Mexico, and Canada, in cars, my own aircraft, and motorcyles, and it was the trip with the motorcycle that gave me the lasting memories of our beautiful countryside.